Materialism and Social Inquiry in the Continental Tradition in Philosophy

Materialism and Social Inquiry in the Continental Tradition in Philosophy

Andrew M. Koch

LEXINGTON BOOKS
Lanham • Boulder • New York • London

Published by Lexington Books
An imprint of The Rowman & Littlefield Publishing Group, Inc.
4501 Forbes Boulevard, Suite 200, Lanham, Maryland 20706
www.rowman.com

Unit A, Whitacre Mews, 26-34 Stannary Street, London SE11 4AB

British Library Cataloguing in Publication Information Available

Library of Congress Cataloging-in-Publication Data Available

ISBN 978-1-4985-5169-4 (cloth : alk. paper)
ISBN 978-1-4985-5171-7 (pbk. : alk. paper)
ISBN 978-1-4985-5170-0 (electronic)

Contents

Introduction

The concept of materialism is as old as philosophy. In pre-Socratic Greece, elements of materialist philosophy can be found in the "atomism" of Democritus and Leucippus. A concern for the material and contextual elements of social practice can be found in the writings of the Sophists. Materialism, in its various forms, continues to interest scholars today.

After a thousand years of slumber during the Middle Ages, interest in philosophic materialism reemerged. Components of the atomism found in Democritus returns in the empiricism of Bacon, Hobbes, and Hume. "Induction" is asserted by Bacon as the means by which the sensations of external reality are turned into claims to knowledge about that reality. Thomas Hobbes asserts that our reality consists of objects in motion, whether animate or inanimate. David Hume argues that only our experiences of physical reality can provide the basis for a claim to knowledge. Sensation is treated by the empiricists as the means by which human beings connect to the material world.

However, there is another thread within the Western tradition in philosophy that questions the purely empirical approach to the issues of knowledge and perception. This is the continental tradition. If the empirical tradition could be characterized as focusing on "sensation," the continental tradition could be said to focus on "cognition." That is, the continental tradition is concerned with how a fact of sense data is transformed into a cognition, or operational understanding of the world for the organisms engaged in acting in the world.

This means that the continental tradition has been concerned with consciousness. Since Descartes's statement, *I think, therefore, I am*, the continental tradition has explored the definition and content of consciousness. The problem is that consciousness is difficult to define. Is it the same as *life*? Is it simply the ideas that we have in our head at any given moment in time? Is it linked to some deeper meaning in either a spiritual or historical sense? Since consciousness is generally thought of as emanating from a realm of ideas, it is often addressed in juxtaposition to the consideration of the concrete material reality that is the basis of sensations.

These question have led some in the continental tradition to develop systems to understand consciousness that have a strongly metaphysical character. Georg Wilhelm Friedrich Hegel developed a system in which human consciousness is tied to the unfolding of universal reason. The process of history and the development of human consciousness proceed together as a spiritual development of the human mind as it uncovers the rationality in history through the exploration of its own consciousness. The objectivity of Hegel's system is assured by both its metaphysical character and post hoc method of validation. The influence of *spirit* is beyond any direct perception, and the evidence of its rationality is demonstrated only in hindsight.

A slightly different, yet equally metaphysical, path is forged by Edmund Husserl. Husserl's phenomenological method seeks to identify a "science" for the study of consciousness in which objective elements of consciousness can be identified within the lived experience of individuals. For Husserl, metaphysics is at the core of the phenomenological method as it provides that domain in which "things in themselves" can be understood by consciousness.

As a result, there is a distinction between the knowledge that is generated by observation and that which is attained by the phenomenological methods. Empiricism legitimates its claims to knowledge through a path that requires repeatability, falsifiability, and observation. But this empirical methodology, according to Husserl, ignores the critical role of life as a precondition for the creation of understanding about the world. Only a living being can have a cognition.

In his criticism of empiricism, Edmund Husserl asserts that the problem with the empirical approach is that it "naturalizes consciousness."[1] What Husserl means by this is that consciousness is treated as a function of the body and its sensations rather than as a transcendental condition of existence. For Husserl, the objects of contemplation can only be understood as manifesting themselves transcendentally within our consciousness. The desk on which I am writing is not literally in my head as I contemplate it. My thought of the desk is, therefore, manifested transcendentally. Thought, ego, intention, and consciousness are elements of life and constitute a precondition to the experience of sensation establishing a basis for Husserl's transcendental idealism.

Numerous criticisms can be made of the phenomenological approach. The subjective and internal nature of phenomenological assertions make it difficult for Husserl and his followers to claim the *science* of their endeavor, even though they assert such a position. Thoughts exist in a reality that is disconnected from the world of experience, history, and culture. The assertions made regarding the character of life and the nature of our phenomenological quest requires a construction of the subject that itself will have historical and cultural roots. There is simply no objective platform from which to make the kinds of assertions that Husserl needs in order to objectify his methods.

These problems occupy much to the efforts of twentieth-century followers of phenomenology as they try to confront these issues. Heidegger, Sartre, Merleau-Ponty, and others try to identify the means by which history and culture have influenced our thoughts and ideas, but they have not fully abandoned the notion of transcendental subjectivity. The work of Michel Henry in *Material Phenomenology* tries to confront this problem by creating a dualism within phenomenology to account for both life and the effects of society.[2] However, even Henry is still struggling with the transcendental character of phenomenology more generally.

This work will focus on another path within the continental tradition. I will argue that one can trace the emergence of a material understanding of consciousness, specifically the *content* of consciousness, in some of the works going back into the eighteenth century. Focusing on Kant, Marx, Nietzsche, Weber, and the poststructuralists, it will be argued that this group of philosophers abandoned the pursuit of defining *essence*, the *thing-in-itself*, with all the metaphysical baggage that comes from such a quest. These scholars create an understanding of cognition from which a form of materialism evolved. Once the metaphysical goal of defining life as a singularity was abandoned, it is possible to formulate a material understanding of cognition and its connection to the lived experience of human beings.

Such a path is still concerned with consciousness. However, this historical and cultural form of materialism holds the position that consciousness is a product of material conditions. However, the consideration of what constitutes a material condition is open to wide interpretation. Is a material condition limited to the configuration of atoms in a given time and location? Do material conditions refer to the state of evolutionary adaptation in the relation between life and the environment? Is it simply the position each person holds as a part of their socio-economic circumstances?

There have been several formulations of such a strategy that have emerged throughout the history of Western philosophy. Generally, this position states that all human knowledge of the external world can be understood as the product of that interaction and the processing of raw sensation into cognitions. The structures and concepts used for the processing of sensation are not innate in the individual but are the products of social conditioning, or the cultural context in which the experiences occur.

Therefore, not only is the notion of transcendent knowledge inconceivable, but any notion of knowledge that is unmediated by context is also undermined. Such a view is associated with a relativistic view of both ethics and epistemology, more generally. Knowledge claims are a human product, the generation of which is stimulated by need, and the results of which are shaped by the contextual order of a given society.

F. A. Lange terms such a materialist position "sensationalism" in his discussion of the Greek Sophists.[3] Protagoras claimed that "man is the measure of all things." This simple statement denies the validity of both unmediated empiricism and the metaphysics that would support the generation of idealist philosophy. The formulation of nature's laws cannot be divorced from the human perceptions in which those laws are articulated. Transcendental claims to knowledge separate themselves from perception and, therefore, do not constitute a valid epistemological base for knowledge claims.

The totality of our environmental experiences establishes the context for the formation and articulation of ideas. Our consciousness is a reflection of the totality of those experiences. The experience of the world is manifold. It includes the activities driven by biological imperatives and the pursuit of food, clothing, and shelter, but also the social interactions that form the basis of history and culture. These would include the social norms embedded with human practices, the technological conditions into which people are born, and the conditions of the natural world that set the parameters for human activity.

These socio-cultural conditions cannot be separated out from the material experiences that human beings have as they are also significant factors in the shaping of consciousness. They direct the construction of a cognitive understanding of the world upon which people act. The subject is *in the world* in a formal sense. What defines the subject cannot be separated from the world. There can be no transcendental character to subjectivity. There is no objective ground on which to stand to construct the transcendental subject.

It is this cognitive picture upon which people act. Its roots are material in a double sense. It is material in the way that material experiences of the world create the content for its formation. It is also material because in acting upon that cognitive picture human beings reinforce the materiality of those experiences. These actions are the material force in history.

This work will treat this materialist thread in the continental tradition as an unfolding of ideas. There is no perfect materialism. There is no fully complete system. However, there is a direction. It is a process in which new insights are built upon the ideas of others within the tradition.

The work will operate on two levels. It will seek to build a model of materialist understanding that will be used as an ideal-type, in the Weberian sense, for comparison to our various epistemological models for the construction of social knowledge. The second task of this work is to demonstrate movement. The methods of social analysis have become more materialistic over the last two hundred years. This has been the result of some specific and identifiable adjustments to the way in which the task of social inquiry has been perceived. Not all of these adjustment have been carried out by scholars generally identified as materialists. Nevertheless, they have contributed something significant to that path of inquiry.

Chapter 1 will construct a model of materialism. What are its central features? How can materialism be discussed in a foundationless world? What does it look like when stripped to its core ideas and basic implications? Chapter 1 will also address the significance of Darwin. With the publication of *The Origin of Species*, Charles Darwin introduced a biological component into the discussion of materialism. The connection between the human organism and the environment, as a determinant in physical adaptation, has a decidedly materialistic tone. Human beings are subject to the same biological processes of species adaptation as all other organisms on the planet. Therefore, the implications of Darwin spread far beyond biology. I will suggest some implications for philosophy, expanding some remarks on the subject presented by John Dewey.

Chapter 2 deals with Immanuel Kant. No one considers Kant a materialist. However, in his discussion of phenomenal knowledge there are significant questions raised by Kant that are important for the development of a materialist understanding of the world. What does it mean to give up the search for *essence*? Where does that leave us in our quest to make sense of the world?

Chapter 3 is a discussion of Karl Marx. It would be impossible to discuss materialism and its relation to consciousness without some reference to Marx. However, Marx should be treated as an opening of the discussion, not its final word. Further, Marx is also important in articulating the material power of discourse. If the content of conscious serves as a person's picture of reality, it will shape their actions. This make the struggle to control discourse a political struggle.

Chapter 4 focuses on Max Weber. Weber is a bit of an enigma, impossible to characterize in any simple fashion. His embrace of data in social science has led some to consider him closer to empiricism and positivism. However, his stress on emotions and empathy have caused others to see him within the fold of phenomenology.[4] Chapter 4 will sort this out and discuss the implications of Weber for the evolution of materialist philosophy.

Chapter 5 explores the ideas of Friedrich Nietzsche. If Kant is the Apollonian builder, Nietzsche is the Dionysian destroyer. Nevertheless, there is something fundamentally materialistic about his approach. It is Nietzsche who begins to ask the questions about what Darwin really implies for our understanding of ourselves and the understanding of consciousness in an age of evolutionary biology.

Chapter 6 addresses the work of the French School known as poststructuralism. Poststructuralism draws inspiration from Nietzsche, Marx, Weber, phenomenology, and existentialism. Often criticized as a *negative* philosophy that seeks to undermine all foundational claims, there is also a strong undercurrent of materialist assumptions that animate its analysis. The chapter will draw on primarily the writings of Jean Baudrillard, Michel Foucault, and Jacques Derrida, but other authors will be mentioned to draw out some of the critical implications.

Following chapter 6, the work will conclude with some brief remarks about materialism as an approach to the comprehension of social and political life.

NOTES

1. Edmund Husserl, *Phenomenology and the Crisis in Philosophy* (New York: Harper, 1965), 82.
2. Michel Henry, *Material Phenomenology* (New York: Fordham University Press, 2008).
3. F. A. Lange, *The History of Materialism* (New York: Harcourt Brace and Company, 1925), 38.
4. John Hall, "Max Weber's Methodological Strategy and Comparative Lifeworld Phenomenology" in *Human Studies* 4:2, 1981.

Chapter One

A Model of Materialism

INTRODUCTION

The world has been transformed by a materialist understanding of our social, political, and cultural reality. In the ancient and medieval worlds materiality played a subordinate role to an overt or implied metaphysical sub-current. Human beings were said to have a mission, a telos of perfectibility in either the Aristotelian or Christian sense. A *purpose* was at the core of the human experience. Such a notion provided the precondition for ethics as well as the organizing principle of science. Scientific knowledge had to reinforce the notions of transcendence for human thought and action in order to be considered legitimate within the larger community.

The result was a series of narratives on the human experience in which the social and political context were asserted as reflections of ontological and teleological essence. Each of these narratives then cloaked itself in claims of transcendence, ordained by God, nature, a static view of human nature, or a naïve view of science. An inalterable view of subjectivity produced a fixed notion of ethics, morals, and social prescriptions, all supported and legitimated by an understanding of epistemology that had transcendentalism at its core.

Thus, even as Plato and Aristotle are replaced by Augustine and Aquinas, the project remains the same. All are seeking to ground their illusive, transcendental claims about human subjects in a way that will sanction their social and political prescriptions for public life. Through those prescriptions, social and political institutions create the conditions for the reproduction of subjectivity in a form that reinforces itself through the conditions for its own generation. As the circle is closed, the illusion of essence is secured as it is claimed to be the sanction of nature, God, or reason itself as a foundational support for proposals on the social order.

In the early modern period the search for transcendental foundations begins a long path of disruption. The conditions of knowledge set down in the course of scientific inquiry cannot be met by the old metaphysics. The result is an attempt to protect the elevated notions of consciousness and reason by isolating their domain from the influences of necessity and mere sensation. "Natural Law" becomes the last stand of the old epistemological/ontological formulation, as proposed by both the empirical (Locke) and continental (Kant) traditions in philosophy.

By the middle of the nineteenth century the old order had broken down and the search began for a new understanding of the relationship between human beings and the knowledge they construct. However, there was a new dynamic in the mix that could not be ignored. This was the work of Charles Darwin and the emergence of evolutionary biology as the model for understanding the emergence of the human species on the planet.

Evolutionary biology changes the fundamental understanding of the human species' relationship to the world. From the beginnings of civilization, the cultural artifacts that have been passed down through history convey a long-standing endeavor to separate the human being from the conditions that affects all other life on the planet. The view is that consciousness makes us different. The ability to engage in self-transcendence makes human beings special. Our materiality was always subordinate to activities of our mind. Whether we want to call it the "forms" or the "noumenal," the implication was the same. Human beings have the ability to enter a domain of reason and understanding that provides them with a special status.

But that is not the world in the age after Darwin. We have long ago abandoned the logic employed by Descartes to demonstrate the proof of God's existence. Imagining the existence of something is not sufficient to demonstrate its being. So it is with all the elaborate fabrications designed to save our unique dignity in a world driven by the fluidity of material existence.

An underlying thesis of this work is that a materialist understanding of social reality has been developing in the social science over the last three to four hundred years. This is a transformation in which even Descartes, Bacon, Hume, and Kant have participated, albeit in incremental ways. The rise of a material understanding of the world has transformed the condition in which social inquiry takes place. The search for the static has given way to the understanding of processes. The transcendence of being has given way to the notion of change and adaptation of biological entities.

The development of this material understanding could not help but have an effect on our understanding of society and politics. Since the beginning of recorded history many of the artifacts of human self-understanding have focused on the legitimation of the status quo. This is the case for both society and politics. Institutional life is constructed to maintain the conditions that gave rise to it. Thus, it does not enact a "truth" but manifests the distribution of status and power in the society. Such a realization means the role and function of democracy has been greatly misunderstood in contemporary political thought.[1]

However, I would not want to give the impression that there is one materialism that has emerged in the twentieth and twenty-first centuries. What has happened is that various paths of social inquiry and emerging disciplines within the social sciences have developed their methodological strategies and underlying ideas to account for increasingly materialistic assumptions. Even within the various philosophic schools there is movement toward a more materialist understanding of the social order. From Kant to Weber, from Marx to Althusser, and from Nietzsche to the postmoderns, all are seeking to refine their methods and assumptions in ways that incorporate a materialist perspective.

The old order has given way. Materialist methods, regardless of their specific origins, all give special deference to the dynamic and contextual nature of all knowledge claims. The idea that human beings organize their social and political existence according to transcendental truths manifested in natural law cannot be sustained. There are simply no means by which such a claim can be validated. In general, materialism transposes the sequence of causality in our understanding of social and political reality. Human beings do not enact transcendent truths as a matter of purpose, but enact the political realities as a matter of concrete law and structure, thus replicating the conditions of their generation. This creates the illusion of universals. Materialism provides a means to analyze the material conditions that gave rise to beliefs and practices, without necessarily giving ethical sanction to those same practices and beliefs. Whether one uses the specific methods of Marx, Nietzsche, Weber, Foucault, or others in this tradition, it is now clear that social inquiry is demanding a connection to materiality for explanations of both the causes and effects of social change.

MATERIALISM AND SOCIAL INQUIRY IN THE CONTINENTAL TRADITION

To say that materialism, as a component of social inquiry, has increased over the last three hundred years is not to suggest that all the various methods of inquiry are the same. For that reason, no simple definition of materialism can be offered. They all engage the slightly different domains of referents. The constitution of material causality varies among different traditions. They differ on the degree to which an idea can be a material phenomenon. The different methods also vary with regard to the attitudes toward what I will call the *scientificity* of inquiry. By that I mean the degree to which the results of inquiry can be called scientific or a "hard fact." These, and other differences, lead to a variety of approaches.

However, what is not in question is the fact that social inquiry has been becoming more materialistic in the assumptions that inform its methods. Some of this can be attributed to the ascendency of the scientific method. The scientific method is constructed around inductive logic as a means to create hypotheses about the world that can be tested for validity. This alters the culture as well as the conduct of science.

Science creates society in which questions must be organized within a certain syntax in order to be explored. The result of this process is two-fold. First, it creates a model for the conduct of inquiry within the phenomenal world. There must be empirical reference points. Statements must be falsifiable in the sense that hypotheses can be amended based on empirical data.

However, the other outcome of the scientific method is that it creates an understanding of the types of questions that can and cannot be answered scientifically. The significance of this distinction should not be underestimated. In this way the use of science and the scientific method not only allows for the relative understanding of the regularities in nature but also creates the conditions where the public can (hopefully) distinguish between matters of fact and matters of belief. This has a transformative effect on the culture and constitutes the source of the distinction between premodern and modern culture.

The continental tradition in philosophy is a fellow-traveler with the positivists that espouse the virtues of the scientific method, but are generally less willing to assert its supremacy with regard to the study of social phenomena. Their view is that when strictly applied to the study of human beings, the use of strict scientific syntax has its limitations. Material science demands empirical reference points. Its interest is in causality and predictability. It has a problem with the analysis of social constructs. They are not things in an ontological sense. The defined patterns of behavior and thus do not lend themselves to the same methodology.

For the continental approach to social inquiry, its empirical reference points are historical and contextual in nature, often buried under numerous interpretations and ideological discourses. Its questions deal with the causal origins of social practices and norms. The task for materialist research in this tradition is to create plausible causal connections that avoid both overt and implicit transcendentals in historical explanation.

While there are achievements in the quantitative and behavioral approach to the study of human phenomena, it often fails to account for its own subjective and interpretive biases. Matters of class and race are often discussed in this regard even though the issue is far broader. Social inquiry tends to reflect the prevailing narratives as the implicit foundation for the legitimacy of its research claims. To operate, such an approach must freeze and circumscribe the identities of what it seeks to explain, fixing in place a narrative about living beings that resides within a dynamic historical process. For late-twentieth-century continental materialists such a shortcut creates the epistemological error of closure.

Society is constructed within a world that is material and empirical, but its dynamics are often manifested on the level of belief. It is for that reason the term "materialism" is not synonymous with "empiricism." The material study of society must incorporate a methodology that allows for an understanding of the material influence on the formation of ideas and beliefs and also provides for a means by which to understand the material force of those same beliefs. If the origin of ideas is not transcendent, then there must be complex causal dynamics in place that are contextual. History, culture, religion, and technology will generate attitudes and beliefs that will inform action. To study those influences has been of greater interest within the continental tradition in philosophy.

This requires that the content of society and culture be treated as social artifacts. This means that the question of the *truth* of cultural beliefs and attitudes cannot be considered. Such a consideration is outside the scope of what materialist methods can accomplish and is considered a matter of ideology. Materialist inquiry is also amoral, in the sense that it cannot advocate the truth of a moral position. All is relative to context. Culture and morality are *indications*, or *symptoms*, of the wider collection of beliefs that move people to actions.

Therefore, when addressing the question of materialist methodologies, some attention must be paid to the means by which ideas are formed. In order to meet the criteria of materialism such an inquiry must be carried out without reference to transcendent subjectivity. This is the point of the genealogical method outlined by Nietzsche and Foucault. It is the direction Marx is heading, although with imperfect execution. It informs Althusser's *Structural Marxism*. It is the objective of Weber's "Logic of Culture Science."

Materialism can be used to uncover the processes by which beliefs are constructed. It aims at social explanation a step removed from the lived experience of those actually engaged in social and cultural reproduction. It is not objective, in the sense of asserting any alternative truth to the metaphysical and teleological elements that animate living culture. It is interested not in presenting an alternative truth but uncovering the relative, contextual beliefs of a society and demonstrating their material origins and the material conditions that sustain them.

In that sense, the approach of the continental tradition is understanding rather than strict causality. As a materialist philosophy it seeks to uncover the processes of lived experience and create an explanation of the dynamic process in which the materiality of experience has produced the conditions in which human beings find themselves today. It must be carried out without reference to a metaphysical plan or teleological agenda. Such explanations must be constructed with the historical artifacts as their empirical reference points. Further, it must be carried out without reference to a static, transcendental assertion of subjectivity.

It is simply a means by which we come to an understanding of the operations of society in a world that has been transformed by the possibility that that human beings have their own story to tell. It is a position with regard to human understanding that starts with the existence of concrete living organisms in the world. It means that they have been part of biological evolution like all the other species on the planet. What differs is their ability to keep a record of their experiences through the generations. For that reason, the influence of Charles Darwin in the discussion of materiality should not be ignored.

CHARLES DARWIN

A discussion of Charles Darwin may seem like an odd place to start a discourse on the methods of social inquiry. After all, Darwin's field of study was biology. It seems like an odd cross-over to suggest that there was significant influence from Darwin in the field of social inquiry and philosophic epistemology.

However, the social impact of Darwin went well beyond biology. Darwin's writing gives impetus to the further development of materialist ideas in the nineteenth century. He is repeatedly referenced in the writings of Marx, Engels, Nietzsche, and others as they formulate their understandings of how human beings come to an understanding of their social existence. Darwin puts the world in human hands. His ideas constitute a transformative moment in the development of the self-understanding of the human experience.

In the span of human history, we need to keep in mind how recent Charles Darwin's theory of human evolution actually is. The systematic exploration of the fossil records in the eighteenth and early nineteenth centuries began to show that there were changes taking place within living organisms over the course of time. This record also generated the idea that the earth was much older than had previously been considered. The origin stories of the human species needed to be made consistent with the historical record.

The fossil record led the biologist William Paley to suggest small changes in living organisms over the span of time. While Paley did not challenge the idea that God had created the world and all its creatures, Paley was important in acknowledging a process of adaptation and change among living organisms.

However, there were some scientists that were moving in a different direction. Alfred Wallace had been working on fossil records in the 1850s and had proposed in a publication in 1855 that the evolution of species was far more extensive than was suggest by Paley. It was clear that Wallace was moving in the same direction as Darwin, and this publication by Wallace pushed Darwin to finish his work, *The Origin of Species*, which he published in 1859.

It would be hard to overstate the significance of Darwin in the development of modern materialist philosophy. The reason for this is simple. With the publication of *The Origin of Species* in 1859, there existed a complete, rational, scientific account of human existence that did not rely, on some level, on the intervention of supernatural forces or an all-powerful deity.

Darwin makes a simple step-wise argument. He states that human beings have bred animals for centuries in order to enhance certain character traits that are beneficial to their human breeders. Isn't it then possible in nature that character traits beneficial to the survival and procreation of the organism would dictate the direction of species development? To this process Darwin assigns the term "natural selection."[2]

Darwin's idea of natural selection meant that there is a natural process by which life adapts and changes to its surroundings. Further, these changes occur as part of a dynamic that has no influence other than the processes found in nature. Life is characterized as a struggle for existence.[3] Variability among species occurs through slow evolutionary adaptation to the environmental conditions. Those best suited to their conditions will pass the character traits on to their offspring. These adaptations are often very small and are incorporated into species variations over the span of evolutionary time.

Darwin's ideas have transformed biology. With the discovery of DNA the evolutionary perspective on the development of organic life became secure. But there is another question. How does evolutionary biology change our understanding of who we are and how we relate to the wider arena of social and political life?

To put this another way, what does all this mean for the development of materialist philosophy? The entire enterprise of philosophy must be reoriented in the wake of evolutionary theory. The issue was addressed by John Dewey at the beginning of the twentieth century.

In 1909 John Dewey gave a lecture at Columbia University entitled, "Charles Darwin and His Influence on Science." In the address, later published as "The Influence of Darwinism on Philosophy," Dewey contrasts the old and new understandings of philosophy. The old view wedded science and morality. Change occurred but change was tied to purpose, end, and telos. Life was assigned a meaning and any alteration in the social or physical universe was tied to the purposes of human existence. As Dewey describes it, to make the physical world intelligible it had to be linked to the theological considerations assigned by idealism and metaphysics.[4]

Dewey goes on to state that in order to progress, science needed to free itself from metaphysics.[5] Darwin is key in that transformation.

> The Darwinian principle of natural selection cut straight under this philosophy. If all organic adaptations are due simply to constant variation and the elimination of those variations which are harmful in the struggle for existence this is brought about by excessive reproduction, there is no call for a prior intelligent causal force to plan and preordain them. Hostile critics charged Darwin with materialism and with making chance the cause of the universe.[6]

Such a paradigm shift in the understanding of the origin and place of the human species displaces the notion that consciousness can transcend its conditions to arrive at universal moral codes or create fixed and stable concepts that are immune from the vicissitudes of material order. Plato's "forms" become irrational conjecture. "Natural law" in the Kantian or Lockean sense is a projection of the Judeo-Christian tradition. Hegel's idealist teleology of consciousness is transformed to a purely speculative enterprise. Darwinian evolution means that the mind is a tool for the successful adaptation of the organism employing it.

> The genetic standpoint makes us aware that the systems of the past are neither fraudulent impostures nor absolute revelations; but are the products of political, economic, and scientific conditions whose change carries with it change of the theoretical formulations. The recognition that intelligence is properly an organ of adjustment in difficult situations makes us aware that past theories were of value so far as they helped carry to an issue the social perplexities from which they emerged.[7]

Darwin brings a materialist understanding of the world that not only decouples science and metaphysics, but also provides us with an understanding of how to read the past. The conditions of social existence must be seen as the product of social, political, environmental, and culture conditions out of which they are formed. From the late nineteenth century to the twenty-first, this is how the materialist understanding of biology transformed our understanding of social and political existence.

Evolutionary biology means that there is no knowledge beyond what human beings create. We are also adaptive creatures that seek to create conditions that enhance our own survival. Further, our understanding of the ideas for our social and political existence have no foundation other than those origins. This not only transforms our self-understanding but changes the methods by which we must come to that understanding. Nothing can be the same in the world after Darwin.

THE ISSUES OF MATERIALIST ANALYSIS

The overarching thesis of this work is that materialism has increasingly become embedded in our understanding of ourselves and the conditions of social existence over the last two hundred years. Even prior to Darwin the direction of philosophy and social inquiry was to rely increasingly on empirical reference points in the creation of knowledge. Darwin's contribution was to provide a biological foundation for the development of those claims.

However, that is not to suggest there is only one materialism or that materialism has an impact on social thought only through one avenue. The suggestion is that there are many materialist elements that can be found in our contemporary understanding of social and political life and that over the last two hundred years we have seen an evolution in thinking about the way in which we understand the social and political context in which we live.

There are a variety of problems in the formulation of a singular approach to a material understanding of the world. There are different opinions on what constitutes materiality in the conduct of research. Is it the case that only objects that can be directly sensed have material presence in the world? Can an idea or concept have material force through its ability to influence the course and direction of human behavior? Along that same line, are all references to concepts themselves metaphysical in nature and, therefore, undermining of any materialist claims? The metaphysical nature of language itself is an area of considerable debate.

Another issue concerns the discussion of life itself. Is the phenomenon of life qualitatively different than other forms of materiality? Common sense would suggest that a rock and a person have different qualities. Can that be captured within a materialist paradigm, or would such an approach generate a metaphysical form of "vitalism?" On the flip side, is it possible to generate a form of vitalism that is not metaphysical in character? A case for a materialist neo-vitalism is explored by Rosi Braidotti in the collection *New Materialisms* edited by Diana Coole and Samantha Frost.[8]

Related to the discussion of life is the issue of consciousness. Is it possible to formulate a notion of consciousness that has a level of material standing, or is it all reduced to subjective introspection? Is it even necessary to define consciousness in order to proceed with materialist analysis? What types of limitations would be associated with such an approach?

Another aspect of consciousness concerns its content. How is the content of consciousness formed? Is it from reason alone? Is it simply the recollection of experience? Is it able to move beyond experience but still retain material origins? This, of course, takes us to the question of will. Materialism generally reject the notion of free will, but is there a consideration of will that can be consistent with materialist philosophy?

Another area that ties together materialist philosophy and social inquiry concerns the extent to which subjective factors impose themselves into the exploration of social phenomena. Is it possible to eliminate subjective factors in our understanding of social and political life? This has been a perennial question in the realm of social research and there have been numerous strategies employed to try and do so. This task points to the fact that various research tools have been developed precisely to make our understanding of the social world conform more closely with the criteria of materialist philosophy.

Finally, are there the limitations of inductive logic itself? As Bacon stated, induction is the means by which new knowledge about the world is generated. Even if one does not adopt the full skepticism of Hume, there are going to be epistemological limitations to the status of what is produced through inductive logic. If elements of Kant's paradigm are brought into the mix, suggesting that we only know the superficial appearances of objects, there are further limits on the status of our claims to knowledge. One is forced to conclude that all claims to knowledge must be limited in their scope and must be hypothetical in nature. All general hypotheses will always depend on the absence of a counterfactual observation. Therefore, it must be a condition of material analysis that "truth" and "universality" be absent from the discourse. (More will be said about that in the next section.)

Because many of these questions cannot be answered definitively, even the rise of evolutionary biology and inductive social science cannot lead to a singular epistemological model or a pure materialist approach. Instead, there has been a steady march to make the realm of social inquiry more materialistic, while at the same time incorporating elements of various philosophic schools along the way.

There can be no perfect materialist philosophy. There is simply too much that we do not know about ourselves and the nature of our physical reality. However, that does not mean that some characteristics that materialist philosophy should incorporate cannot be determined. In the wake of Darwin, Nietzsche, Freud, existentialist philosophy, empiricist philosophy, Marxism, and poststructuralism, it is possible to make some observations about what a general model of materialism should incorporate.

THE BOUNDARIES OF MATERIALISM IN SOCIAL INQUIRY

There are a variety of ways in which elements of materialism have been incorporated into social inquiry. These include positions on truth, ontology, historical dynamics, causality, and subjectivity. It is also important that the notion of evolution be somehow represented in any model that has materialist leanings. Hence, any system asserting materialist credentials must have elements that are dynamic and open to change and transformation.

What follows is a simple list and explanation of some of the elements of materialism that can be found. The ideas contained in this section are not designed to be an all-inclusive definition of materialism. Rather, the purpose is to give some general guidelines of what should be generally expected in the formation of a model of materialist analysis in social research. In any analysis it is necessary to start somewhere, and the guidelines that follow are designed to take a step in that direction. In that regard, they will guide much of the analysis and critique that follow in the subsequent chapters.

1. The centrality of the human body for the conduct of inquiry must be acknowledged. What this means is that a materialist understanding of the world must take into account the instrument that is doing the inquiry and making the claims to knowledge. The general nature of this assertion allows for elements of both empiricists and continental traditions, acknowledging that neither can give a complete account of the system of knowledge and its formation. Empiricism fails to give an adequate account of the difference between sensation and cognition. Neo-Kantianism can be too static in its characterization of human faculties and too universalist in its understanding of reason. But all must give some recognition of the physicality of the human body.

Another issue related to this is the question of mind-body dualism. Elements of this understanding can be found in the Christian tradition and have their home in philosophy in the writings of Descartes and Kant. However, taken literally, it cannot be formulated in a fashion that is consistent with materialism.

Mind-body dualism must be understood as a heuristic device in the history of Western philosophy, a tool for making distinctions between thought and sensation, but a concept that has no ontological status. Therefore, it is not a useful concept in the discourse on human beings and the knowledge they produce. The brain must be treated as part of the body, and the activities of the brain must be addressed in relation to the body's physical existence. This means that the activity of the brain cannot be afforded transcendental status.

2. *Reason* is a social construction. Therefore, the content of *reason* must be treated as historically and contextually constructed. Western philosophy since the time of Plato has given enormous attention to the subject of reason. It is asserted to be the capacity that separates us from the other animals on the planet. It is that special faculty that allows for the creation of civilization, universal morality, and infinite progress among the human species.

But it must be acknowledged that the behavior that is considered reasonable has taken a variety of forms throughout the ages. Reasonable action cannot be separated from the context in which it is performed. Summoning gods that control the climate may be reasonable behavior for a people without a modern understanding of weather. Democratic political practice may be reasonable for people who have assumed a basic equality of rational faculties among the populous.

The point here is not that climate science is equivalent to the summoning of gods or that autocratic rule provides the same amount of legitimacy for collective action as democracy. The point is that in each of the conditions in which those actions take place there is a supporting narrative that makes the behavior rational *in its context*. Rationality must be understood in a fashion that is less universalistic and static than is often the case. As Max Weber points out, what we call rational may also directly relate the efficient pursuit of the ends we are trying to achieve. This claim is directly related to the next point.

3. The only epistemological position compatible with materialism is relativism. By relativism I mean much more than the usual philosophic debates surrounding moral absolutism and relativism. This relativism encompasses not only that debate but also sweeps up both Paul Feyerabend's epistemological relativism and Thomas Kuhn's notion of paradigmatic change. Our understanding of the world falls within the domain of what is possible for us to know at a point in our historical development. Thus, knowledge will be constructed in a way that is consistent and compatible with the dominant epistemological paradigms of the day. This relates directly to points four and five.

4. Everything we know is human-centric in character. We can have knowledge of only that which we can sense and process. The knowledge we produce is constructed within the limitation of the human organism and is constructed in a fashion that serves human interests. We do not go beyond those limits. To suggest that we can arrive at universals surrounding the truths of nature, society, or ethics through such a limited process is to stretch the limits of our sensibilities.

Further, it is only relativism that can address the dynamic nature of our human and environmental systems. History as a dynamic system has been discussed in relation to an overarching teleology by Hegel and others. However, such grandiose blueprints for humanity only fix an interpretation of the present onto an evolving and fluid future. There is simply not enough contextual stability for such an enterprise to have much authority.

In that sense, the development of philosophic systems constitutes the artifacts of the intellectual journey of human beings. They chronicle changes in human thinking about who we are and the quality of our actions. But all that knowledge is about our journey as a species, not knowledge more generally. Thus, all such claims should be interpreted as part of the archeology of the species, signposts, and symptoms of their changing character.

5. There can be no valid claims to universal knowledge in either the natural or social sciences. The reasons for this are manifold. In the natural sciences, all products of inductive logic are hypothetical and subject to falsifiability. This is not to suggest that there are not experiences of *facts*. If I let a pencil drop to the floor it is possible to call the event a repeatable and observable fact. However, the simple observation of facts is only part of the inductive process of natural science. The question of science is whether it is possible to discern a general rule that governs repeating observable phenomena. Here the matter is more complex and requires the act of *interpretation*. When one asks by what operation or rule the dropped pencil falls to the floor, one requires the mental activity of interpretation. Aristotle's physics is replaced by Newton, and Newton by Einstein. Inductive logic leaves open the possibility of new data and information that transforms the entire understanding of scientific research. There is simply no escape from the act of interpreting, even in the natural sciences.

In philosophy and the inquiry into social activity, the case for interpretive understanding of the knowledge seems more evident. If there were one religious, ethical, philosophic, or social system that had properties that were obvious to all human beings it would not be an insurmountable obstacle to formulate a universal social structure to which all could subscribe. The problem is that universal systems must depend on numerous assumptions in order to create closure. Questions of being, free will, the power of reason, the discourse on equality, and the role of power and conditioning in human experience have made the articulation of foundational support for universal systems impossible.

Within the span of the human intellectual enterprise this leads to two conclusions. First, the assertion of universalist systems is constructed upon a priori assumptions that themselves lack foundational validity. Second, the construction of such systems are, in fact, a posteriori claims that reflect the historical conditions and distribution of social influence and power in a given age. Universal systems seek to capture the illusive essence of the human experience, but their actual affect is to reify the moment in which they are formulated.

This means that in any formulation of social and political prescriptions there will be a mix of *facts* along with contextually driven assumptions and subjective factors that will set the tone and direction of the analysis. History may be influenced by objective factors, but the interpretation of history is still a human enterprise. Therefore, one of the tasks of materialist analysis is to sort out what can be distinguished in these different domains.

Such a view of the role subjective elements and interpretation play in constructing our social knowledge has a long history in the continental tradition in philosophy. Kant raises it in *The Critique of Judgment*. Weber talks about it in *The Methodology of the Social Sciences*. Nietzsche discusses the matter in numerous places. The poststructuralists describe the process in which the illusion of closure occurs. The point is that within this tradition there has been a general trend. As the systems these authors have constructed reflect a greater commitment to materialist epistemology, the more they have embraced the idea that the knowledge constructed by human beings is interpretive rather than transcendent and universal in character.

6. Ethics must be viewed materialistically and pragmatically. Materialism implies a certain level of ethical relativism, but that does not mean that norms of human behavior cannot be formulated on a pragmatic basis. It simply means that the supporting discourse for prescriptions about human behavior must avoid transcendental claims regarding a deity's wishes, natural law, a construction of human nature, or speculation about the intent or structure of a hypothetical natural order.

An example of this pragmatic conception of ethics can be found in the prohibition on murder. It is still possible to construct a social prohibition on murder without reference to God's commandments or reference to natural law. Even Hobbes understood that human beings will seek to create the conditions for their own survival, and the prohibition on murder can be placed within that category. If society is necessary for human beings to thrive, then some restrictions can be placed in the actions that would undermine the social order. If murder were to be unconstrained by social prohibition it would be impossible to form the communities in which human beings survive and thrive. It is for this reason that as the complexity of human society increases, there is a tendency for the actions that direct human behavior to become more pronounced.

While materialist analysis may not be able to address that issue and assign a value judgment regarding this trend, it can do two other things that will be beneficial. First, it can help in the formation of those rules and procedures that would be beneficial to human social functioning and survival. Second, it can provide a means to examine social prohibitions with the intent of eliminating those that do not have pragmatic grounding.

The pragmatic grounding of ethics does not require a transcendent or universalist claim to knowledge. It does require that the rules governing conduct have some relation to the benefits of their consequences. An example can be demonstrated in the rules governing driving an automobile. It is necessary to choose whether a citizenry drives on the right-hand side of the road or the left, not because it can be related to a universal law of driving, but because of the horrific consequences that result from no societal agreement.

The point here is not to suggest that all ethical matters can be decided this way but to promote an understanding that ethical prescriptions must have a foundation in the benefits they generate for the survivability of the human beings under their domain.

7. Subjectivity is socially constructed. The problem of defining human nature as the foundation for political prescriptions is as old as civilization. However, all of these attempts have shared the methodological dynamic under which they have operated. Plato reacts to the democratic state under Pericles. Locke addresses the rise of the owning classes. Marx defends the interests of the working class during the rise of mass industrialization. Each asserts a model of human subjectivity consistent with its ideological position. Each is a product of its time and circumstance.

Further, each of these formulations of subjectivity empowers a mode of existence for the society. In doing so, the rules that govern human conduct are organized in a fashion that will reproduce as many of the external environmental conditions of that mode of existence as possible, as well as create the legal and normative structures that will reproduce the ideological conditions that maintain the order. This is point explored by Louis Althusser as well as the poststructuralists.

It is for this reason that the influence of power and its distribution must also be considered in the matter of social inquiry. The institutional order reproduces the conditions for its existence. One of the ways it does so is to define the character of human beings in a way that is consistent with the institution's exercise of power. To cite one example, the state makes a distinction between citizens and non-citizens. In doing so it also assigns itself power to enforce those distinctions and to assign a set of expectations that is attached to that identity. There is no gene that makes one a citizen of any country; it is a historical product of power and the processes by which human civilization has evolved.

8. What we can say about human beings with some certainty is that they are adaptive. Darwin assigns such a characteristic to all life and produces the empirical evidence to support it. Life adjusts to its conditions. But change is not the same thing as progress.

For Darwin, the adjustments to the environment take place as part of a process of natural selection. It is a biological process in which species' mutations that enhance survivability manifest the alteration of species. While the evidence suggests that human origins also followed this pattern, it is not how patterns of social change are normally addressed.

Societal change should be seen as a process of problem solving. Human beings are driven by biological imperatives, but in modern society these are carried out within a setting that is social. In that sense, problem solving must include: the satisfaction of material needs, the search for social arrangements that provide safety and security, and the formulation of institutional practices that are seen as legitimate for what Jürgen Habermas calls the societal "steering" decisions.

Societal change may not always be positive. In part that depends on the time frame and environmental factors. However, the assessment of the positive or negative nature of change will also be influenced by ideological factors, ideas, and beliefs that are divorced from a materiality of conditions. In this regard, the notion of change and adaptation should not be equated with "progress." Progress is a popular idea and is a central component of early Enlightenment thought. But the definition of progress is much harder to pin down. In philosophic terms, it is an idea that is wedded to a teleological or ideological conception of past, present, and future that is often influenced by subjective considerations. Further, in Darwinian terms, "progress" would suggest we knew the end or goal of evolution. Such a position is not possible within a materialist framework.

9. Ideas and ideologies may have material force in history and may direct social change. Material necessity is an important matter in the consideration of social change. An important step was taken by Karl Marx in articulating this position. The fact that human beings must continually reproduce the conditions that satisfy their physical needs is certainly an important factor in shaping our societal practices. However, even with his commitment to deciphering the influence of material necessity on the societal condition Marx will admit to the material force of ideas and their revolutionary potential. [9]

Does Marx follow through on the importance of this concept? In part he does, but in part he does not. He does in the sense of that it is outlined in *The German Ideology*, in which the formation of consciousness is linked to the totality of material experiences in society in which he includes the ideological and culture conditions. He does not in the sole focus on production as the source of all ideological and culture factors in society.

The point here is that ideas may have a material link to other ideas as part of a cultural history that is transmitted from one generation to the next. Even though ideas do not possess extension in space, and do not possess materiality in that sense, they may still exert material influence on the direction of collective action. For example, Max Weber pointed to the influence of religion in the Middle Ages as directing action without a direct link to the material forces of production. Ideas and ideologies form part of the material context in which human beings find themselves. In a society which possesses formal mechanisms to transmit culture practices and societal norms from one generation to the next, and where there exist extensive social institutions whose very existence is predicated on the propagation of certain modes of belief, it would seem unwarranted to exclude such considerations from a material analysis of history.

Such a view increases the complexity of social analysis. Material analysis must include a consideration of the mechanisms by which ideas and culture influence the direction of societal change. Ideas must be part of an understanding that includes all the factors leading to the formation of identity and consciousness as the totality of human consciousness is the force that directs history, not just the parts linked to material necessity. The work of Louis Althusser attempts to move Marxism more in this direction. However, it is the writings of Friedrich Nietzsche and the poststructuralists that adopts this position more directly.

10. Questions surrounding the nature of human existence can be engaged as part of an evolving discourse on the materiality of life, in its various forms. Evolutionary biology continues to develop as a field of scientific research. The light it sheds on our self-understanding has already been significant, albeit, often misunderstood. From this perspective, weak ontological notions about the nature of human beings may be possible. What is not possible are any suggestions of teleological paths, assertions regarding the meaning and purpose of existence, or religious pronouncements.

To some degree, this leaves open some space for a materialized form of neo-vitalism. Living things have a different quality of existence than a rock or a pool of water. This work will not address neo-vitalism directly, even though there has been some new interest in the topic expressed in the literature. The reason is that most of the authors taken up in this work will weave some elements of what it means to be a living being into their philosophic systems. Living cannot be divorced from sensing and having cognitions.

CONCLUSION

As mentioned above, there are no perfect materialist philosophies. The definition of materialism itself is problematic which is why it is better to treat the philosophic systems according to their unique characteristics rather than just build a single model of materialism. This work will focus on identifying the materialist elements in the philosophic systems reviewed.

The point of this work is to suggest that social inquiry has been becoming more materialistic for the last several centuries. Increasingly social research has sought to develop methodologies that can account for human conduct within the limits of material explanation. Different schools of thought have produced different methods, but they all continue to move in the same direction.

This has particularly been the case as scientific achievements have been wedded to developments in philosophy. Empirical science has transformed our world. It has provided new technologies and in the process transformed the material conditions of existence. In that sense, it has reinforced the process of development of materialist methods in social research.

In this sense, Darwin is a metaphor for the paradigmatic shift taking place in our self-understanding. This is an understanding that cannot be divorced from the ideas of materialist philosophy that Darwin, empirical science, and, increasingly, the domain of social inquiry have come to support.

However, such a correspondence with empirical science is not as simple as it may appear. What seems like a direct route, the paths taken by empiricism and positivism, are not without their problems. Positivism cannot easily account for the complexity of subjective factors in the domain of social inquiry. It does not account for the reciprocal interaction of subject and object in the activity of lived experience. It also tends to shortchange the material force of ideas and ideologies as substantial factors in explaining social change. Hence, the matter of consciousness and the formation of consciousness cannot be divorced from the account of material force in history. Ideas and culture are not corporeal. They do not lend themselves to the syntax of science, except in a limited fashion. Human behavior may lend itself to empirical analysis but the full range of question surrounding the forces that transform history is more complex and illusive.

The continental tradition in philosophy is more sensitive to this complexity than the empirical tradition. It has generated conceptual tools that assist in our understanding of how the full range of material forces manifest themselves in social change. Semiotics, genealogy, and deconstruction are forms of material analysis that have furthered our understanding of the ideological components of consciousness and how they are transmitted. In that way, they further our grasp of the material origins of human identity and the influence that has on behavior.

However, even with all these advances it is difficult to conclude that all the questions can be answered and all the problems solved. Part of the problem lies in the fact that the system of language itself has a metaphysical character. The common sense understanding of language is that it *represents*. The word stands in for the object, always implying that the sign captures that illusive "thing in itself," even while leaving the description of *essence* as a statement deferred.

The point is to step back and take a look at the larger picture, the conditions in which our self-understanding can be wedded to transformation in the human story.

What follows will be a critical examination of the works of Kant, Marx, Weber, Nietzsche, and the poststructuralist. The focus will be on the elements of their methodological systems that contribute to a materialist understanding of social research. The work will also identify areas in which their writing move in a different direction than was outlined in this chapter. However, as was stated at the beginning of this chapter, the enterprise of social inquiry has sought to become more materialist over the last several hundred years. The attempts of these authors has been testimony to that process.

NOTES

1. For a discussion of democracy in the postmodern world see *Democracy and Domination* by Andrew M. Koch and Amanda Gail Zeddy. (Lanham, MD: Rowman and Littlefield (Lexington), 2009).

2. Charles Darwin, *The Origin of Species* (Philadelphia: University of Pennsylvania Press, 1959), 163.

3. Darwin, 144.

4. John Dewey, *The Influence of Darwin on Philosophy* (New York: P. Smith, 1951), p. 67.

5. Dewey, 56.

6. Dewey, 11-12.

7. Dewey, 68.

8. Rosi Braidotti, "The Politics of Life Itself and New Ways of Dying," in *New Materialisms*, edited by Diana Coole and Samantha Frost (Durham, NC: Duke University Press, 2010).

9. Karl Marx, "Contribution to the Critique of Hegel's Philosophy of Right," in *The Marx-Engels Reader*, edited by Robert Tucker (New York: Norton, 1978), p. 60.

Chapter Two

Immanuel Kant, Materiality, and the Mediated Experience

INTRODUCTION

Immanuel Kant's legacy is enormous. He has influenced epistemology, moral theory, existentialism, and poststructuralism. His ideas have been criticized, reworked, expanded upon, and vilified. Whether one agrees or disagrees with the Kantian system, it is a model of our reality that cannot be ignored.

What is striking in the philosophic literature is the wide variety of labels assigned to Kant. He is called an idealist, a rationalist, and a transcendentalist, along with a variety of variations on those themes. What he is never called is a materialist. It is not my intention to make such a claim in this chapter. However, it is my intention to claim that Kant was a pivotal figure in the rise of materialism within the continental approach to the social inquiry.

Kant's significance to the emergence of a materialist model of social inquiry is in the doors his philosophy opens. The role of cognition in the construction of human knowledge, the extent and limits of our knowledge, and the subjective character of judgment are but some of the few avenues that Kant explores. These ideas have been reworked and developed by others over the last two hundred years. It is possible to criticize Kant, to reject his system and its ideas. What it is not possible is to ignore him.

This chapter will begin by exploring some of Kant's predecessors. This will accomplish two tasks. First it will establish the epistemological context that Kant will draw on, react to, and argue with, in the development of his own model. Kant has an agenda, but that agenda can, in part, be found in the dynamics of the intellectual debate engaged by Kant's immediate predecessors.

The second matter that can be addressed by this strategy is to introduce one of the dynamics for this work as a whole. The continental tradition in philosophy shares some common elements with the empirical and positivists schools. However, there are also some significant differences that are highlighted by the way in which Immanuel Kant responds to the empiricist David Hume. Some of those differences highlight the more far-reaching distinctions between the two traditions in philosophy and are worth noting here. Sir Francis Bacon and David Hume will be presented as representatives of the empirical tradition. Rene Descartes will be discussed as a predecessor to Kant from the continental tradition.

Following that discussion, I will briefly summarize the three projects that occupied Kant's writings; knowledge of nature, the conditions for moral prescriptions, and the issue of human judgment. Kant calls the works on these topics "critiques," but they are really explorations of the conditions that are necessary to the formulation of knowledge within each sphere. This is what is so radical about Kant's approach. He explores the conditions of knowledge rather than making positive assertions about the world itself. This is the cornerstone of his "Copernican Revolution" in philosophy. The Kantian system seeks to outline a meta-theory about the rules and conditions of knowledge more generally. In that sense, Kant's general intent will be echoed in the works by Hegel, Marx, and the poststructuralists.

The chapter will conclude with an analysis of Kant's work in the light of the materialist model outlined in chapter 1. There are quite a few areas in which Kant could never be considered a materialist. However, by opening a discourse on the limits of human understanding, the mediate condition of knowing, and the subjective character of judgment, Kant is beginning to open the door for a materialist understanding of the world. Kant does not walk through that door. However, others do.

THE CONTRAST:
CONTINENTAL AND EMPIRICAL TRADITIONS

It took hundreds of years for the development of materialist forms of social inquiry. It was dangerous to espouse some of the concepts necessary for the development of materialism at the end of the Middle Ages. It could lead to banishment, imprisonment, or worse. However, materialist philosophy had a fellow traveler, empirical science.

Empirical science is not exactly the same as materialist social inquiry, but the success of empirical science in explaining recurring patterns in nature and providing a means to harness nature forces for production allowed for the acceptance of scientific explanations of the world and its processes. There was an affinity between the rise of science and a materialist form of social inquiry. This led to the development of an epistemological model in which there was less emphasis on religious and teleological explanations of the world. Tension existed between metaphysics and the emerging scientific method, and the intellectual space for an alternative understanding of how to conduct social inquiry began to emerge.

The anti-transcendental character of the scientific outlook provided room for a new avenue of questions regarding the nature and character of social and cultural life. In ancient Greece there was little distinction between the metaphysical question of the "right form" of social life and the study of the exiting conditions of the social order. The transcendental was fused with the analysis of the contemporary social order. The case was similar during the Middle Ages. The moral was synonymous with the *true*, and the telos of implementing God's plan became the work of the philosopher/theologian.

The opening for a new understanding of social inquiry requires a new epistemological outlook. Bacon, Descartes, Hume, and Kant all move in the direction of defining new assumptions and new methods about what human beings can know. And, while each separates his ideas from the epistemology of the Middle Ages, each shares a concern about the limitations of human understanding. Each raises some doubt about the expanse of the mind's ability to know, while outlining a means by which we can extend ourselves to those limits. In carrying out this formulation we are reminded of both the material substance of the world as the central issue of knowledge and the materiality of our own presence in the world.

These figures outline many of the problems with which nineteenth- and twentieth-century philosophers must grapple. What is the nature of knowledge? Can we define being? How can we arrive at ethical conduct and codes of human behavior? All of this must be carried out within an intellectual environment that is increasingly suspicious of metaphysical explanations of social and physical reality.

Sir Francis Bacon

Some of the first systematic works of the modern age on the matters of science, understanding, and materialism can be found in the writings of Sir Francis Bacon (1561-1626). In the "Great Instauration" and "Novum Organum" Bacon discusses both the problems of the old form of knowledge and outlines a methodology for the scientific method. Both essays convey the necessity of moving into a greater materialist understanding of the world.

Coming out of the Middle Ages it was clear that the epistemological methods employed were not providing human beings with a means to generate a greater and more accurate understanding of the physical environment. As Bacon puts it, " . . . what is now done in the matter of science there is only a whirling round about; and perpetual agitation, ending where it began."[1]

Logic applied to the world seems only to perpetuate falsehoods.[2] There is a tendency to defer to traditions in the study of things rather than employing methods that will generate new knowledge.[3] New ideas are often ridiculed and rejected by a population that prefers simple answers.[4]

Bacon's point is that there is need not just for greater knowledge of the physical world, but that this can be accomplished only by using a different methodology for the construction of knowledge. This is to be carried out with the employment of two strategies: the use of an alternative form of logic, and a more rigorous program of observation and experimentation. This requires engaging the material of the world directly as an object and not treating nature as if it were only the reflection of some divine plan.

Bacon repeatedly refers to the use of syllogistic reasoning as part of the old thinking about science and the world. Syllogistic reasoning, or deductive logic, relies on the authority of some accepted truth in order to generate new claims to truth. Such thinking, claims Bacon, is useful for clarifying arguments and terminology. However, this logic has several flaws. First of all, it contains the implicit danger of perpetuating falsehoods.[5] If one of the premises in the syllogistic argument is false, then the conclusion will also be false. For that reason, Bacon makes it very clear that he does not accept "tradition" as the proper validating mechanism to a claim to knowledge. Real progress comes from tearing down traditions when they can be proven false.[6]

But to Bacon the biggest flaw in deductive reasoning is that it cannot formulate new knowledge about the world. Beginning with accepted truths means that deductive logic can only extend the description or character of an already accepted knowledge claim. Therefore, Bacon asserts that the new method of knowledge construction must employ inductive logic. Induction can generate new knowledge. It does not rely on tradition or the repetition of accepted truth. Instead, it begins with the observations of material reality.

Inductive logic in the sciences begins with the observation of phenomena. Information from the senses may be sifted and examined in many ways.[7] The sense impressions are then analyzed by the intellect for indications of regularity, causality, or other conditions that provide some new information about the object and its relation to other objects in the world. Empirical and rational faculties are employed in this analysis.[8]

Relying on sense impressions for the generation and verification of knowledge claims provides the scientific enterprise with a means to validate claims to knowledge that are not subjective in character. Further, because sense impressions have their origin in the observation of what can be observed in the material environment it is possible for others to observe the same phenomena. Through this process claims to knowledge can be accepted or rejected within a wide community of observers. Bacon refers to this process as "demonstration."

Therefore, providing a new method opens up a new path for the creation of knowledge. We must begin again.[9] All the past claims must be reexamined. We must begin with sense impressions of the material world and employ a systematic examination of nature in a careful and deliberate way.[10] Induction is a form of knowledge construction that "upholds the senses."[11] Where the senses seem inadequate to the task, instruments and experiments can be employed to further our understanding.[12]

By asserting the significance of sense impression in the demonstration for claims to knowledge Bacon helped push our philosophic understanding of the nature of knowledge in a new direction. Sense impressions, cognitions, and testable hypotheses are now the means by which we can make claims to knowledge. Material reality takes center stage. Religion is given a nudge toward the realm of the irrational, even as Bacon "prays" that the knowledge of things human will not "interfere with things divine."[13]

René Descartes

The contrast between the world of human knowledge and the realm of things divine is also found in the work of René Descartes (1596–1650). But Descartes is closer to what will be called the rationalist school of philosophy than Bacon. Descartes relies on a dualism between that which is part of the realm of the divine, accessible through the use of reason, and that which is the realm of physical reality. According to Descartes, we know that there is a God because "nothing cannot be the cause of something."[14]

But Descartes is also looking for a new path to knowledge of our physical world. Like Bacon, he rejects deductive logic as a path forward. It simply will not provide us with any new knowledge about the world.[15] The truths it has produced are mingled with errors. What is needed is a new method that allows the sorting of truth from error. All things must be doubted so that we can put our understanding of the world on a new foundation. Begin with simple facts and move to more complex ones in a systematic way.[16]

However, Descartes's solution interjects the idea of consciousness into the process of understanding. Descartes asserts a dualistic philosophy that distinguishes the activities of consciousness, the mind, from the senses in the exploration of the physical world. The methods employed are, therefore, also different. For the exploration of the mind, there is only consciousness exploring itself. For an inquiry into the nature of physical reality the senses serve as the initiator of understanding.[17]

It is possible to have knowledge of cause and effect in the world.[18] However, this is only the case for the realm of the senses and only in a limited way. The senses cannot tell us the essence of an object, but can tell us only what may be useful or harmful in an object.[19]

The senses may also deceive us. Sensation assigns more substance to rocks than to air. The senses tell us the earth is flat rather than spherical.[20] For this reason Descartes says that we need to both train ourselves with an understanding of the physical world and to recognize the difference between sense impressions and cognition.

Sensations initiate our understanding of the world, but the sensations are turned to understanding only once they have undergone the process of reflection. At this stage in our understanding, sensations move from body to mind. Descartes's point is that the mind has certain capacities to process sensation that turn it from pure sense impression to understanding. The mind implicitly knows the character of extension in space and time.[21] The mind has the capacity to process ideas of quantity, division, substance, and voids.[22]

Descartes remains a central figure in the development of modern philosophy. However, his ontological dualism may raise a question about his centrality in the rise of materialism in the Western world. A realm of pure thought and consciousness leaves open the possibility for speculation about non-material causality in the world. This critique is softened, somewhat, if we accept that Descartes is struggling with the role and status of consciousness even as he is trying to overcome the biases of deductive inquiry coming out of the Middle Ages.

Therefore, even as Descartes would not be considered a "materialist" in any formal sense, he is helping to set in motion a path of inquiry that stresses a methodical inquiry into the physical conditions that surround us. In Descartes's statement that we cannot know the essence of physical objects he is effectively denying the possibility of transcendent knowledge in the realm of experience. This claim effectively challenges both the ethical teleologies of ancient philosophy and the transcendentalism of Christianity as it applies to the physical conditions of the world.

He tells us to doubt what we know. Then it is through our conscious, meticulous, and systematic inquiry into those conditions that we can formulate a body of knowledge that serves human needs. An inquiry into the nature of matter and our material environment is an important component of Descartes's focus.

David Hume

David Hume (1711–1776) is a major figure in the development of empiricist philosophy and an important philosopher of modernity. He is also a critical figure in moving a form of materialist philosophy to the center of philosophic debates.

Hume claims that all knowledge is from sensation. Human beings have no innate ideas.[23] The ideas we have are a compilation of sense impressions, as they are stored in the human memory.[24] Ideas are formulated out of these sense impressions, but as Hume states, while sense impressions are strong and immediate, ideas are more distant and subject to the influence of sentiments and creative fantasy.[25]

> Nothing, at first view, may seem more unbounded than the thought of man, which not only escapes all human power and authority, but is not even restrained within the limits of nature and reality. . . . But though our thought seems to possess this unbounded liberty, we shall find upon a nearer examination that it is really confined within very narrow limits, and that all this creative power of the mind amounts to no more than the faculty of compounding, transposing, augmenting, or diminishing the materials afforded us by the senses and experience.[26]

At this point Hume has already demonstrated a certain level of materialist credentials. However, he is going to examine the implications of these simple concepts and explore the consequences for knowledge more generally. Metaphysics and religion cannot be demonstrated with reference to sense impression and are therefore relegated to irrational superstition.[27] Morality is argued to be a sentiment that is largely the product of cultural conditioning. Therefore, any notion of morality that is asserted to be the eternal and immutable principles of transcendent reason is rejected.[28] Morality must be treated as relative to custom and culture. Morality is a feeling rather than something that can be considered as hard immutable fact.

But Hume is going to go further, raising doubt about our ability to have knowledge at all. He carries out his epistemological critique by strictly adhering to the empirical principles he presents. He claims that cause and effect among physical objects is something the mind "infers" from the association of two conditions with one another. We do not directly experience causality. To do so would violate the material premises of empiricism.[29]

Hume also challenges the epistemological validity of the inductive enterprise outlined by Bacon. Statements of fact always have the possibility of error.[30] Since inductive reason relies on the direct observation on the part of the subject, there may be a domain of objects not considered in the formulation of truth claims. Further, since inductive statements are predictive of future conditions, conditions that have yet to be experienced, the results of inductive logic are not factual but probable. Therefore, the products of inductive reason are probabilistic hypotheses based on past experiences but, in a strict empirical sense, cannot be asserted as factual. The same results will only appear if all the conditions surrounding the event are similar.[31]

There is little doubt that Hume furthers the scope and significance of materialism as a philosophic position in modern epistemology. His demands for empirical referents in claims to knowledge and his claims that science is hypothetical and probabilistic set the parameters for the modern understanding of science.

However, Hume is less adept at expressing the materiality of subjective experience. Hume states that the science of man is the foundation for all other sciences and sets himself the task of defining its character. Nevertheless, while denying the notion of "innate ideas" he comes close to such a claim in defining the "capacities of the mind" in the essay, "A Treatise on Human Nature." In the work Hume discusses our limited ability to conceive of infinity,[32] our ability to contemplate being and non-being,[33] our understanding of proportionality, among other capacities of the human mind.[34] Here Hume may be closer to Kant and the "categories" than is often discussed. To put it another way, Hume's analysis shifts from a subject-object relationship to a subject-subject introspective inquiry. Is Hume breaking his own rules for the construction of knowledge? A case could be made to support that conclusion.

THE KANTIAN SYSTEM

Along with Hume, Immanuel Kant (1724-1804) is one of the giants of modern philosophy. In contrast to Hume's skepticism, however, Kant tries to create the epistemological conditions for the generation of knowledge without the baggage of Hume's skepticism. Kant's project is to define not what we know but the conditions that must be present if we are to make knowledge claims in the areas of natural science and universal morality.

Following Descartes, Kant employs a dualistic strategy, dividing our explorations into the realm of physical sensation (phenomenal) and the realm of thought and the mind (noumenal). However, the simple dualistic approach is not sufficient to overcome Hume's critique. Kant must rely on claims of transcendental reason in order to create the space for his two domains of knowledge. As Kant explained, experience alone is not enough to generate a claim to knowledge. Experience is a species of knowledge but understanding requires a set of rules that must be presupposed prior to the generation of knowledge.[35] Kant's three critiques, *The Critique of Pure Reason*, *The Critique of Practical Reason*, and *The Critique of Judgment*, are the attempts to lay out those rules for their particular domains of inquiry.

Knowledge of the Physical World

In his analysis of knowledge in the phenomenal realm Kant set out by reorienting the relationship between subject and object. In Hume's empiricism, knowledge is asserted to be a direct result of stimuli received through the five senses. Human beings are claimed to be blank slates upon which the record of sense impressions are imprinted. The experiences can be recalled from memory, and human creativity may draw from the recurring patterns to generate statements about the phenomenal realm. For Kant, such a position leads to an unrelenting skepticism regarding the possibility of generating any knowledge about the world.

In response Kant makes two critical moves. In qualifying sensation as the initiator of knowledge rather than assigning it the quality of knowledge itself, Kant is then able to argue that the process of knowledge construction is more complex than that described by Hume. Taking his lead from Aristotle and Descartes, Kant argues that human beings possess a set of faculties for processing simple sensations and transforming raw experience into cognitions. Kant called these faculties the *categories*: quantity, quality, relation, and modality.[36] The important point in this discussion is not whether this list of faculties is exhaustive. The central point is that in Kant's view the human mind mediates between the objects of experience and the generation of knowledge claims about the physical environment. To state it simply, the human being can sense only what the senses are capable of sensing, and the cognitions of the human mind are limited to those that are the products of the faculties for cognition. Therefore, the relationship between subject and object is transformed.

Kant touched on the implications of this in the preface to the second edition of *The Critique of Pure Reason*.

> Hitherto it has been assumed that all our knowledge must conform to objects. But all attempts to extend our knowledge of objects by establishing something in regard to them a priori, by means of concepts, have, on this assumption, ended in failure. . . . If intuition must conform to the constitution of the objects, I do not see how we could know anything of the latter a priori; but if the object (as object of the senses) must conform to the constitution of our faculty of intuition, I have no difficulty in conceiving such a possibility. . . . For experience is itself a species of knowledge which involves understanding; and understanding has rules which I must presuppose as being in me prior to objects being given to me, and therefore as being a priori.[37]

Here Kant is laying the foundation for his second critical claim regarding knowledge of the physical world. However, he must begin by preparing the foundation with regard to the possibility of a priori statements. Kant asserts that the conditions for cognition must be present prior to the formation of knowledge claims about the objects of the world. We know this a priori. We know that the possibility of a priori knowledge exists, claimed Kant, because there are things that we can say about the condition of an object prior to its perception.

In the introduction to the *Critique of Pure Reason*, Kant made his case for the possibility of a priori claims. Pure reason is the exploration of what we can know a priori.[38] He asserted that this is not knowledge of objects but the mode of knowing objects. In an exercise to prove his point, Kant imagines taking away all sense data from an object. He then asks, is there anything that we can know about the object without direct experience? His answer is that we can know a priori that it must be extended in space and time.[39] Thus, a priori knowledge is possible.

Having laid out the foundation for the existence of a priori knowledge, Kant is ready to make his next significant statement about our knowledge of the physical world. There is a distinction between the world that exists in itself and the world as it appears to human beings. The logic is simple. Human beings have five senses with which to sense the world of objects. There are four categories of faculties that are used in the formation of cognitions about the world. We know, a priori, that objects must have other characteristics that are not the result of our direct experience, for example, their extension in space and time. Kant concludes that it is similarly rational to assume that there are other properties of objects that do not conform to the limited sensing apparatus of human beings.

His conclusion is that there may be many other characteristics that make up the totality of an object's existence which are hidden from our perception. The full array of an object's potentiality must be regarded as an issue of metaphysics. An object's "essence" must be considered as a subject of speculation, not empirical fact. The "thing-in-itself" is beyond the scope of human inquiry.

Therefore, human knowledge is confined to the appearance of objects, not things-in-themselves.[40] Nevertheless, when we consider objects we must understand them as things-in-themselves, even though their essential character is beyond our perception. Otherwise, "we should have landed in the absurd conclusion that there can be appearance without anything that appears."[41] Rationally, we know the totality of the object is behind its appearance to us, even though we only know the surface of the object's totality.

Kant asserts that the phenomenal world is driven by causality and necessity. Our senses are the window into that reality. However, they cannot provide us with the essence of that reality. Not only do the senses give us incomplete data, they also provide us with only the surface impressions of a reality that is beyond our human grasp. Reality is an infinitely complex array of causality that is beyond our abilities to fully discern. Further, what we do understand is the result of a process of cognition in which sensations are mediated by the faculties present in the human mind.

So while Kant gives us something, knowledge of the physical world, he also takes something away. We are separated from the world, knowing only its appearance. We have no ability to approach either its infinite richness nor its metaphysical essence. What we claim to know must always be within the confines of what is humanly possible.

With all of his transcendental assertion regarding the scope and limits of knowledge about the world of objects it would seem that Kant is far removed from anything that can be called a materialist philosophy. However, in *The*

Critique of Pure Reason, Kant has set in motion an understanding of knowledge of the physical world that does meet some of the criteria for materialism set out in chapter 1. By limiting the scope of human claims to knowledge Kant has addressed the human-centric nature of knowledge claims. More will be said about this later.

Kant's Moral System

The Kantian epistemological system for the study of nature explores the conditions that must be present in order to make claims to knowledge of the physical world. In that phenomenal realm there are recurring patterns of relationships that are governed by the laws of causality and necessity. However, that is only one part of the Kantian formulation.

Kant was also concerned with elaborating the conditions that must be present for the formulation of universal codes of morality and ethics. In seeking to avoid the relativism that emerges from Hume's empiricism, Kant must confront an epistemological problem. How is it possible to construct a foundation for the elaboration of moral codes in light of the parameters that Kant erects for his understanding of knowledge more generally?

Kant realized that in order to avoid a relativistic morality, any elaboration of moral codes must be unaffected by experience. Therefore, the path to morality must operate according to different epistemological parameters than are found in the construction of knowledge of the physical world. As a dualist, Kant builds on the Cartesian idea of a separation between the realm of objects (the phenomenal world) and the realm of ideas (the noumenal). Such a distinction would seem to provide a basic structure for the construction of such claims. However, Kant recognizes a problem.

The problem for morality is highlighted in a discussion found in the introduction to *The Critique of Pure Reason*. In the introduction, Kant makes a distinction between two types of statements: analytic and synthetic. In an analytic statement the predicate is contained in the subject.[42] We make such statements in order to clarify concepts or give definitional content to the words in our expressions. "A bachelor is unmarried" is such an analytic statement.

In synthetic statements the predicate is not contained in the subject. It adds something new to the understanding of the object. In the statement, "the pencil is yellow," new information is added to the discussion of the pencil. While Kant exempts mathematics from such restrictions, he stated that all other synthetic statements are posteriori.[43] They can only be made after experience.

The problem, of course, is that the noumenal realm does not lend itself to direct observation. It suffers from the same limitations of metaphysics more generally. To advance, it needs synthetic statements that add knowledge to the discourse. However, metaphysics operate outside the realm of experience. To advance knowledge in metaphysics would require the elaboration of synthetic a priori statements. In *The Critique of Pure Reason* this leads Kant to conclude that there are questions that are beyond our ability to provide definitive answers. A few of these are addressed at the end of the work, in a section called "The Antinomies."

Human beings have senses through which they have contact with the empirical world, but also "[they] must reckon [themselves] as belonging to the world of the mind, of which, however, [they have] no further knowledge."[44] Lacking a synthetic a priori in the noumenal realm upon which he can construct a universal moral system presents Kant with a problem. This forces Kant to ask the questions of morality differently. Therefore, the first question is not, "what is moral behavior?" The first question is, "what conditions must be present if we are to be able to consider the possibility of universal morality?"

Kant's answer is simple. Autonomy of the will is the supreme principle of morality.[45] To Kant, morality is about the assessment of intentional behavior on the part of individuals. However, to be held accountable for one's behavior a person must be free to choose an alternative. If the will were simply the product of cause and effect, operating according to necessity, the consideration of morality would be no different than the assessment of cause and effect in the physical realm. But such a position would deny the possibility of morality as Kant defined it, all together.

Kant knows that he does not have the ability to demonstrate the autonomy of the will. Such demonstrations would require the illusive synthetic a priori. Autonomy of the will must be assumed in order to make morality possible.

Kant also states that the assessment of the outcome of our behavior is not a perfect measure of moral action. The world is an infinitely complex web of actions and reactions. Every act sends a ripple through that web of causality, influencing the occurrence of other events and behaviors. There is no certainty that an action with moral intent will produce only positive consequences. Further, it may not be possible to say what constitutes the good without the consideration of the specific circumstances in which moral questions arise. For that reason Kant states that there is nothing that can be said to be "good" without qualification except "good will."[46]

Is there a principle that can ensure the universality of actions of good will? Such a principle is contained in the *Categorical Imperative*. "Act only on a maxim by which you can will that it, at the same time, should become a general law."[47] So the first condition that must be met in the consideration of moral acts is whether or not they can be universalized for all people in all times and all places.

The second condition of morality deals with practical matters of moral intent. "Act so as to treat man, in your own person as well as in that of anyone else, always as an end, never merely as a means."[48] Kant called this the *Practical Imperative*, as it is to serve as a principle for individuals as they interact with one another. It is to serve as a guide to the creation of a social order directed by reason in the conduct of people's daily lives.

Several issues are clear from the Kantian model of morality. It is clear that Kant views each individual as an independent moral agent. He is, in that sense, an ontological individualist. Freedom of the will means that each individual possesses the ability to make moral choices that transcend conditions and circumstance. For that reason, the individual's intentions form the centerpiece of moral considerations.

Kant's Categorical and Practical Imperatives are the transcendental framework for the generation of universal content regarding moral behavior. Thus, it is clear that Kant outlines a framework in which human reason is sufficiently robust that universal moral principles can be formulated as *natural law*. Reason informs the techniques for moral understanding.

For Kant, the legal system is a direct result of his system of moral reasoning.[49] As reason informs the creation of universal moral codes, so it also creates the guidelines for positive law. Laws, to the extent that they are legitimate, must be constructed in a way that is consistent with the universal laws of freedom and morality.

The Kantian moral system has been extremely influential in the two centuries since its formulation. However, any assertion that it is "materialistic" would stretch the limits of credulity. Kant's entire moral system has a transcendental character, and even the twentieth-century attempts to soften those claims by people like John Rawls do not solve the problem. Not only is the system built on the stated assumption of free will, but there are several other assumptions in the mix. Kant is also assuming the universality of reason and its moral pronouncements, but also the equality of reason, in the sense that the same processes and conclusion can be arrived at by all people in all places and times. Such a claim ignores the relative nature of history and context.

Judgment: The Aesthetics of Inquiry

The Critique of Judgment is a work which is often discounted or underemphasized in the corpus of Kant's writings. However, *The Critique of Judgement* opens up a significantly different line of thought in the Kantian project. The work's pronouncements are, in many ways, less rigid and definitive than the structures that govern his two previous critiques. Kant opens up the possibility of individual subjectivity regarding acts of judgment, even as he is trying to outline a priori conditions for the activity of judgment. This is particularly pronounced in the discussion of aesthetic judgment.

Like the other *Critiques*, *The Critique of Judgment* is interested in the question of human knowledge. However, this is again not a question of what we know, but the conditions that must be present if we are to make a claim to knowledge. "Properly speaking the Critique, which deals with what our cognitive faculties are a priori capable of yielding, has no field in regard to objects; for it is not a doctrine, but merely investigates whether and how a doctrine may be possible, considering our [mental] faculties."[50]

At play throughout *The Critique of Judgment* is the juxtaposition of nature and freedom. Kant viewed the faculty of judgment as link between the philosophy of nature and the philosophy of morals.[51] The intellect prescribes a priori laws for the analysis of nature as an object of sense experience. Reason prescribes a priori laws that follow from the condition of freedom.[52] Judgment is the activity that links the intellect and reason.[53]

Kant goes on to say that judging is not only linked to our cognitive faculties but also the power of our imagination. It is related to what Kant calls "spiritual faculties" that include feeling of desire, pleasure, or displeasure.[54] This feeling is particularly manifest in relation to aesthetic judgments.

> If we wish to discern whether anything is beautiful or not, we do not refer its image to the object by means of the intellect with a view to knowledge, but by means of the imagination acting perhaps in conjunction with the intellect we refer the image to the subject and its feeling of pleasure of displeasure. Therefore the judgment of taste is not an intellectual judgment and so not logical, but is aesthetic – which means that it is one whose determining ground cannot be other than subjective. Every reference of images is capable of being objective. . . . The one exception to this is the feeling of pleasure of displeasure. This denotes nothing in the object, but is a feeling which the subject has . . .[55]

So while an image or object may be empirical, the feeling it provokes is entirely subjective. In an aesthetic judgment the image is referred wholly to the subject and to its "feeling of life – under the name of the feeling of pleasure or displeasure . . . " Kant continues, "this forms the basis of a quite separate faculty for discriminating and estimating, that contributes nothing to knowledge."[56]

So for Kant, aesthetic judgments are not connected to the ways of human knowing. Aesthetic judgments do not provide us with knowledge of the world or our moral actions. The beautiful and the sublime are matters of subjective taste and refer to the feelings that are produced by our contact with objects rather than our analysis of an object's empirical properties. A feeling of pleasure or displeasure regarding an object, therefore, must always be posteriori.[57]

Nor do aesthetic judgments employ reason, as is the case with the philosophy of morals. They are manifestation of will as desire, and as such, relate to life as a subjective, internal feeling rather than life as the pursuit of knowledge or moral action. It is, therefore, a subjective phenomenon a priori.

What Kant seems to close off in *The Critique of Pure Reason* and *The Critique of Practical Reason* finds a place in *The Critique of Judgment*. Judgment is not connected with knowing but with feeling. It is associated with life as a subjective existence in which individual matters of taste and feeling manifest themselves.

Here Kant has opened the possibility that part of consciousness is not a direct result of reason and intellect. It means that there are experiences that effect the human being that are not directly related to the explanation of empirical phenomena or the explication of the logical applications of freedom. However, the question that follows is a simple one. How large is the domain of judgment? Does it expand if the Kantian systems for empirical knowledge or moral prescription are denied?

KANT AND MATERIALISM

The Kantian system is extraordinary in its scope and depth. However, the question remains about the extent to which there is anything within the Kantian formula that can be considered materialistic. Following the model for materialism outlined in chapter 1 it would appear that there is little evidence that Kant would meet the criteria for materialist philosophy. Kant's entire project is based on the idea that it is possible to establish a priori principles that provide the foundation for the construction of knowledge claims regarding the inquiry into nature and morality.

So much of Kant's scheme is based on the distinction between mind and body that treating the claims as a heuristic arrangement cannot be possible. It is at the very core of the entire system. It allows Kant to establish different models of epistemology for the generation of knowledge claims.

In the discussion of morality, this means that the experience of individuals in their daily lives will have no impact on the content of ethical and moral claims about the world. Kant fully understands that the introduction of experiential influences into the formation of morality leads to moral relativism. He wishes to avoid relativism in morality. Instead, Kant claims that ethical and moral claims are the product of reason, a logical extension of the freedom presupposed as a condition of the noumenal.

But here Kant is assuming a lot more than freedom of the will. The transcendental character of the entire discussion of morality has pushed Kant to assert the universality of reason, denying it any contextual content whatsoever. In application, the moral transcendentals suggested by Kant are so general and so vague that they would not be of much use, especially when two principles come into conflict. For example, in Kant's discussion of the

Categorical Imperative, he suggests that suicide would be a violation of nature's principle of self-preservation.[58] But what of the freedom to die with dignity if stricken by a painful debilitating disease? The problem is exacerbated when such principles are to be the source of law and social policy.

In the end, Kant's moral system is so rigid and universalist in its conclusions that it presents the danger of reifying a historical formulation of morals and setting itself on the course to correct any outliers. This kind of homogenization would fail to account for the experiential factors that have led to the formation of ethical systems that have worked for societies, both past and present. The point is that the practical imperative, in itself, may present a civilizing principle. However, the transcendental claims regarding the origins of moral prescriptions suggest a full denial of experiential foundations. The basis of a prescription may come from its pragmatic function. Its *morality* of the claim may be the afterthought.

As suggested, Kantian dualism and the subject of morality within that dualistic philosophy are problematic when it comes to a discussion of materialism. However, in the discussion of the phenomenal realm the results are more mixed. Kant still cannot be labeled as a materialist, but there are some assertions that have pushed the direction of social inquiry in that direction.

In the discussion of empirical knowledge Kant sets the limits on what is possible. Part of this relates to the issue of transcendental a prioris, but part of this discussion has more practical implications. In making a distinction between experience and cognition Kant is moving in the direction of establishing the human-centric character of empirical knowledge. The categories are faculties of cognition. Even if one were to treat the categories as unfinished and open, the general point remains. Human beings are capable of formulating knowledge claims only within the array of faculties at their disposal. As a result, all claims to empirical knowledge must be bracketed, understood as the claims to knowledge from the position of the human organism, rather than knowledge more generally.

Given the finite nature of human experience it is not contrary to materialism to suggest that all our positive statements about the qualities of an object must be treated as incomplete. In fact, it is a central claim of the materialist approach that the assigning of identities to objects, as well as people, must be assumed to be open to amendment and addition. Kant's claim regarding our inability to know a thing-in-itself has an admittedly transcendental character; however, as a practical matter, the result is the same. It is simply not possible for a finite organism to assign an infinite array of possible identities to an object.

This position also takes philosophy away from a discourse on metaphysics and into a realm that is more materialist in its intent. The mind does not conform to the objects of experience, but the objects of experience are understood to conform to the capacities of the human organism. Therefore, our understanding of the world is mediated by faculties of cognition. Not only does this separate the Kantian model from the empiricist tradition in philosophy, it opens up a discourse that will provide a basis for the emergence of twentieth-century philosophies such as phenomenology, existentialism, and poststructuralism. Each of these has materialist components within their subtle variations.

Another area in which the Kantian system opens a path for a materialist understanding of the world is in his discussion of judgment, especially aesthetic judgments. Judgment is the bridge between the intellect and reason. It is a bridge that takes place within the living human being. Therefore, it must include some experiential component, as the individual is part of a lived historical experience. Kant limits the subjective components of judgment to matters of aesthetics but such a claim may have broader implications. For example, if, as Nietzsche claimed, our relation to the world is an aesthetic, interpretive relationship, then the domain for aesthetic judgments goes well beyond the limit placed upon them by Kant. [59] Such a view leads Nietzsche to a materialist and human-centric understanding of knowledge more generally.

CONCLUSION

It was not the aim of this chapter to give a materialist reformulation of the Kantian epistemology. My attempt has simply been to show the areas in which the Kantian system has provided ideas that will be relevant in the development of materialist methods as Western thought has moved deeper into modernity.

Kant is trying to identify the objective conditions for the subject's understanding of the world. His assertion is that there are such conditions. To identify them requires a level of abstraction. There are rules that govern knowledge construction but are themselves outside the normal validating mechanisms for any specific claim to knowledge. In that sense, they operate on a meta-theoretical level, describing what would be necessary for the formation of the kind of knowledge Kant seeks rather than trying to tell us what that knowledge is directly.

In that meta-theoretical sense, Kant is engaged in an enterprise that is not unlike Marx's *German Ideology* or Foucault's *The Archeology of Knowledge*, albeit with a different objective. Kant wants both causality and necessity in the empirical world. He also wants universal morality. Those objectives directed his project. However, that is not sufficient grounds to assert the truth of his system. That is a different matter altogether.

Kant gives the continental response to the question of knowledge. He does not believe that the claims of empiricism can provide either of the objectives he seeks. The empiricist account of the subject—object relationship does not account for the mediated nature of cognition. In contrast to the mechanical process suggested by empiricism, Kant puts the human being at the center of knowledge construction. The mind does not conform to object, but objects conform to the possibilities presented by the mind and its ability to create cognitions.

Kant's discussion of the human limits of cognition and the subjective character of aesthetic judgments will provide avenues for the development of materialist thought well into the twentieth and twenty-first centuries.

NOTES

1. Francis Bacon, "The Great Instauration," in *The English Philosophers from Bacon to Mill*, edited by Edwin Burtt (New York: Modern Library, 1939), 6.

2. Bacon, "Great Instauration," 10.

3. Bacon, "Great Instauration," 9.

4. Bacon, "Great Instauration," 8.

5. Bacon, "Great Instauration," 10.

6. Bacon, "Great Instauration," 9.

7. Bacon, "Great Instauration," 17.

8. Bacon, "Great Instauration," 12.

9. Francis Bacon, "Novum Organum" in *The English Philosophers from Bacon to Mill*, edited by Edwin Burtt (New York: Modern Library, 1939), 25.

10. Bacon, "Novum Organum," 27.

11. Bacon, "Great Instauration," 16.

12. Bacon, "Great Instauration," 17.

13. Bacon, "Great Instauration," 12.

14. Rene Descartes, *A Discourse on Method* (New York: Dutton, 1941), 172.

15. Descartes, *Discourse*, 15.

16. Descartes, *Discourse*, 15.

17. Descartes, *Discourse*, 168.

18. Descartes, *Discourse*, 174.

19. Descartes, *Discourse,* 200.

20. Descartes, *Discourse*, 194.

21. Descartes, *Discourse*, 200.

22. Descartes, *Discourse*, 200-210.

23. David Hume, "An Abstract of a Treatise of Human Nature," in *On Human Nature and the Understanding*, edited by Antony Flew (New York: Collier-Macmillan, 1971), 291.

24. Hume, "An Abstract," 298.

25. David Hume, "An Inquiry Concerning Human Understanding," in *On Human Nature and the Understanding*, edited by Antony Flew (New York: Collier-Macmillan, 1971), 36.

26. Hume, "An Inquiry," 34.

27. Hume, "An Inquiry," 28.

28. Hume, "An Inquiry," 30.

29. Hume, "An Inquiry," 48

30. Hume, "An Inquiry," 47.

31. Hume, "An Inquiry," 57.

32. Hume, "An Abstract," 182.

33. Hume, "A Treatise," 185

34. Hume, "A Treatise," 191.

35. Immanuel Kant, "Preface to the Second Edition," *The Critique of Pure Reason* (New York: Modern Library, 1958), 16.

36. Kant, *Critique of Pure Reason*, 72.

37. Kant, "Preface to the Second Edition," *Critique of Pure Reason*, 16.

38. Immanuel Kant, "Introduction," *The Critique of Pure Reason* (New York: Modern Library, 1958), 36.

39. Immanuel Kant, "The Critique of Pure Reason." In *The Philosophy of Kant*, edited by Carl Friedrich (New York: Modern Library, 1977), 27.

40. Kant, "Preface to the Second Edition." *Critique of Pure Reason*, 20.

41. Kant, "Preface to the Second Edition." *Critique of Pure Reason*, 20.

42. Kant, "Critique of Pure Reason." In *The Philosophy of Kant*, 30.

43. Kant, "Critique of Pure Reason." In *The Philosophy of Kant*, 33.

44. Immanuel Kant, "The Metaphysical Foundations of Morals," in *The Philosophy of Kant*, edited by Carl Friedrich. (New York: Modern Library, 1977). 197.

45. Kant, "Metaphysical Foundations," 187.

46. Kant, "Metaphysical Foundations," 140.

47. Kant, "Metaphysical Foundations," 170.

48. Kant, "Metaphysical Foundations," 178

49. Immanuel Kant, *The Metaphysical Elements of Justice* (Indianapolis: Bobbs-Merrill, 1965), 45.

50. Immanuel Kant, "The Critique of Judgment," in *The Philosophy of Kant*, edited by Carl Friedrich (New York: Modern Library, 1977), 268.

51. Kant, "Critique of Judgment," 265.

52. Kant, "Critique of Judgment," 280.

53. Kant, "Critique of Judgment," 269.

54. Kant, "Critique of Judgment," 269.

55. Kant, "Critique of Judgment," 284.

56. Kant, "Critique of Judgment," 285.

57. Kant, "Critique of Judgment," 297.

58. Kant, "Metaphysical Foundations of Moral," 170.

59. Friedrich Nietzsche, "On Truth and Lies in a Nonmoral Sense," in *Nietzsche Selections*, edited by Richard Schacht (New York: Scribner/Macmillan, 1993), 51.

Chapter Three

Historical Materialism

The Marxian Tradition

INTRODUCTION

Karl Marx died on March 14, 1883. In the speech delivered at Marx's graveside Friedrich Engels compared Marx to Charles Darwin, citing the parallels between Darwin's discovery of the "law of development of organic nature," and Marx's discovery of the "law of development of human history."[1] Engels goes on to describe how Marx's law of history asserts that the material existence of concrete human beings is the starting point for the analysis of history, placing the production of food, clothing, and shelter as the determining factors in the creation of politics, art, religion, and science.

Whether one accepts the deterministic relationship Marx describes between the base and the superstructure, there is something fundamental afoot regarding methodology that will influence both Marxist and non-Marxist thinkers for generations to come. Marx did not seek to ground his analysis in a definition of human nature, historical teleology (at least at the origins of analysis), or national character. As a methodology, Marx sought to determine the causal linkages between what he saw as two concrete historical facts: the way in which human material needs were met and the social and political institutions that exist.

For this reason, Marx is a revolutionary, but not necessarily for the reasons most often attributed to him. There is something fundamentally different in the method regarding the conceptualization of how human beings come to an understanding of the physical environment and how that process circumscribes both the limits of knowledge and the possibilities of action.

Is Marx the final word on materialism? Such a claim could be defended only within a crude form of economic determinism, one that would not do justice to the depth of Marx's analysis nor the significance of Marx's contribution. Marx is an opening, a leap forward, but to treat his system as the conclusion of the development of materialist methods would undercut a larger and more valuable project, the development of a human-centered understanding of the structures which human beings have constructed.

This chapter will survey the writings of Marx for what is both stated and implied regarding materialism as a methodological and philosophical position. Particular attention will be given to the incorporation of biological and empirical elements in Marx's socio-historical form of materialism. In the latter part of the chapter, emphasis (some might argue too much) will be placed on some of the shortcomings, implicit assumptions, and inconsistencies in Marx's form of materialism. Marx is breaking new ground, but he lacks some of the conceptual tools to formulate a stronger materialist position. To put it another way, Marx wants to conform to the syntax of science developing in the middle of the nineteenth century. That means that he wants to employ inductive logic coupled with empirical reference points for the generation of causal statements. Such a strategy for the study of human culture is not without its limitations. The chapter will conclude with some comments about the legacy Marx left and its influence on materialist philosophy in the twentieth and twenty-first centuries.

HEGEL, FEUERBACH, AND THE MATERIALIST TURN

Hegel

As was discussed in the previous chapter, some of the foundation for the development of a materialist world-view can be found in the writings of Immanuel Kant. The materialism is not in Kant's dualism, transcendentalism, the categorical imperative, or in his formulation of human subjectivity. It has its roots in the question. If human beings are to claim knowledge in the realms of science and morality, what conditions must be present? In doing so, Kant has made answering the question a human-centered enterprise. Further, by relying on the human-centered nature of the question to direct his inquiry, Kant also tried to address the limits on what we can know, moving metaphysics into the realm of the speculative rather than the real. "Essence" is, therefore, removed from our epistemological lexicon.

But such a state of affairs is not universally accepted. The German Idealist tradition reacted to the Kantian philosophy by reasserting the importance of the "idea" within the mind/body dualism of the Kantian system. Central to this philosophy as it comes to Marx is the figure of Georg Wilhelm Friedrich Hegel.

Hegel wants to overcome the mind/body dualism of the Kantian system. He does so by giving preeminence to the development of consciousness as part of a teleology of reason. If our goal is to get knowledge of the Absolute, that is, the world as it "truly is," we must understand the relationship between knowledge and the absolute.[2] To Hegel, thought and being cannot be separated as is suggested by the Kantian system. There must be a unity in order for the mind to be able to contemplate the world. That is, consciousness can only contemplate the objects which are made available to it by the level of its own development. In this way, Hegel tried to close the gap between knowledge and consciousness. This gap, as one would find in the Kantian system, would lead us to the conclusion that, "the Absolute stands on one side, and that knowledge on the other side . . . "[3]

At its core, Hegel's philosophy suggests that the world is ordered by reason and that the unfolding of our consciousness reveals the order of that reason. But Hegel is going to go further. Consciousness, nature, and reality are all ordered by spirit, an underlying rationality that moves dialectically toward self-consciousness. To Hegel, spirit stands in relationship to its opposite, matter.[4] Its sole truth is freedom.

In history, spirit reveals itself as concrete reality. Universal history belongs to the realm of spirit.[5] Spirit makes itself objective in history and the object of thought.[6] It manifests itself in the culture of people, each with its own collective character. Human history is shaped by this teleological movement that is manifested in the collective, historical monuments of human consciousness. Stages of development are negated as new levels of self-consciousness are achieved.

Feuerbach

Like Marx, Ludwig Feuerbach was one of the Young Hegelians in Berlin during the first half of the nineteenth century. Hegel's influence can be seen in the earliest work of Feuerbach, *The Essence of Christianity*, where he speaks of God as an outward projection of the inner character of human subjectivity. However, by his 1843 work, *Principles of the Philosophy of the Future*, Feuerbach's materialist credentials are front and center. To Feuerbach, God is an expression of human reason, reason that expresses the expanse of its own ability to conceptualize the externalization of itself. To put it another way, the qualities given to God are the qualities of reason.[7] The doctrines of religion that express God's essence are really expressions of human essence.[8]

For that reason, Feuerbach asserted that religion needs to be read anthropologically.[9] However, what Feuerbach was claiming is not necessarily what anthropologists today would view as the exterior study of human behavior, etics, but would be closer to an externalization of subjective experience, emics. What Feuerbach missed was the subjective character of speculative philosophy more generally and the problems it would present for a more systematic materialist doctrine.

Therefore, even with his materialist turn away from strict Hegelianism, Feuerbach never leaves it all behind. Feuerbach still spoke in terms of consciousness and human essence as if they are fixed and transcendental expressions. Feuerbach treats the content of reason and consciousness as if they are independent of sensation and experience, trying to free consciousness from the confines of the body. Reason wants to express itself beyond the confines of sensuality. " . . . [T]he essence of reason is disclosed to us primarily in the infinite being."[10] Even if that expression of the infinite is an expression of human sentiments, it still represents the externalization of the transcendent character of reason itself.

Sensation and consciousness are treated as different categories of activity in the mind. Something is real only to the extent that it exists as an object for consciousness. Hence, consciousness is the true reality.[11]

In his 1845 critique of Feuerbach, Marx stresses the problems of that characterization of consciousness. To Marx, Feuerbach is too close to the Cartesian and Kantian view in which consciousness treats the world as an object of contemplations.[12] For Marx, this position implies a passive relationship between the actions of individual subjects and the world of which they are a part. Therefore, consciousness still maintains a transcendent character within the structure of Feuerbach's thought.

Further, by assigning so much autonomy to consciousness Feuerbach disconnects it from the world of sensual activity.[13] Such a position presents two problems for Marx. First, it allows for the creation of a definition of human essence that is not intimately connected to material and historical conditions. Second, the decoupling of sensual activity from the formation of thought and consciousness implied a disconnect between material conditions and the formation of a historical and revolutionary consciousness that is tied to production and residual activity in the superstructure. Marx's entire revolutionary project relies on the strength of that connection.

MARX

It is my contention that Marx's materialism has three distinct phases, the period of the *1844 Manuscripts*, the period of the *German Ideology*, and the period of *Capital*. Each represents a different focus, and a different methodological approach, to the study of social phenomena. Therefore, each characterizes the relationship between material experience and the generation of knowledge about the physical world and its recurring patterns in a slightly different way. Marx is searching for laws of social development that resemble the structures of laws in the natural sciences. While the topics discussed are done so with varying degrees of materialist pedigree, the intent is always to move in the direction of natural science.

Another facet linking all three phases in Marx's writing is the attempt to integrate the notion of "life as activity" into the analysis. I would argue that this is one of Marx's notable accomplishments in the discussion, as it brings human beings into a dynamic process of history. Marx and Engels repeatedly criticize empiricism for approaching the study of human beings and social relations within the framework of what they see as an outdated subject/object dichotomy. Marx repeatedly states that life is activity, an interaction between the living individual and the external environment of which he or she is a part. Hence the problem that Marx confronts is to formulate a description of the process by which human beings come to knowledge within the syntax of modern science, that is, to formulate causal statements about the social world, but to do so in a way that accounts for the dynamic of living beings as part of the process of knowledge construction.

To Marx, strict empiricism does not account for the interaction of living beings with the world. Empiricism must confront the world as "object." It operates by listing the properties of things. To do so, the identities of things must be represented as both closed and stable. Therefore, the accounts of human activity within the empiricist framework do not have the dynamic aspects of historical transformation that Marx wants to incorporate.

One of Marx's great achievements is to begin a conversation about this very problem. While not the final word on the subject, Marx transforms our understanding of the complexity of the study of living, conscious beings that are simultaneously both subject and object. One of the arguments of this chapter will be that Marx's own strategy seeks to synthesize the epistemological requirements of empirical science with the remnants of Hegelian phenomenology after it has been turned right side up. This formula will have a profound effect on the methods for the study of human beings well after Marx's passing.

THE THREE THEMES IN MARX'S WORK

The 1844 Manuscripts

There is much that is appealing in *The Economic and Philosophic Manuscripts of 1844*. The reader gets an account of the mechanism by which capitalism exploits wage laborers, a discussion of capitalism being driven by greed and avarice, as well as pronouncements about the how the emancipation of the working class is the key to the emancipation of all human beings. However, the *1844 Manuscripts* represent the weakest account of materialism in the three phases of Marx's analysis.

The work's most materialist passages are in the brief remarks Marx makes about consciousness and life activity and the role played by production in the securing of human needs. Introducing a theme that will be developed in later writings, Marx asserts that consciousness is shaped by activity in the world.[14] This activity may be scientific, productive, or consumptive, but all of these activities shape our understanding of the social character of our self-understanding. If our understanding of the world is the result of activity, then, the explanations for the rise of political economy that imagine "fictitious primordial conditions" to explain the origin of private property and privately held production must be metaphysical in character. Marx refers to them as "theology."[15] The reference is clearly aimed at Locke and the contract theorists of the eighteenth century. It is surprising here that Marx is not more forceful in asserting the ideological and historical character of bourgeois consciousness in the *1844 Manuscripts*, tying the emergence of liberalism with the rising political power among the owning class.

However, Marx follows this statement with what he calls "an actual economic fact" that connects individual workers to the structures of capitalist production.[16] In capitalist production the worker is turned into a commodity, such that the more productive labor power is, the less the individual worker is worth.[17] In later works, this is the point at which Marx stresses the economics of surplus value and the significance of supply and demand in the determination of wages. But in the *1844 Manuscripts*, Marx develops a different type of argument.

Much of the *1844 Manuscripts* is normative in character and far less materialistically oriented than many of Marx's other major works. It is the case that directly after the discussion on the commodification of labor, Marx moves into a discussion of the estranging or alienating features of the workers' experience within capitalism. As the labor performed by the worker belongs to another, it becomes alienated from the worker.[18] Labor loses its force as an expression of the worker and becomes an alien product to satisfy only the external needs of food, clothing, and shelter.[19] Through the commodification of labor, the worker is alienated from nature and estranged from the character of the human species.[20] The worker is also estranged from other human beings as the labor in which the worker is engaged is actually directed by another who holds control over him.[21] Later in the *1844 Manuscripts* Marx adds the division of labor as one of capitalism's alienating features.[22]

In no other place in Marx's body of work is the topic of alienation taken up in such detail. The terms "alienation" and "estrangement" are mentioned as parts of other discussions, but nowhere with the kind of elaboration and detail as in the *1844 Manuscripts*. The problem is that "alienation" is simply not part of a materialist argument. This might explain why the draft of the *Manuscripts* was abandoned.

To be alienated, one has to be alienated from something. In this discussion Marx repeatedly returns to the idea of human essence[23] or terms like "species life."[24] The problem is that these are terms that do not fit very well with a materialist analysis. They imply closed objective criteria in which there are self-evident sets of characteristics. Historical analysis, especially an analysis based on the idea of an historical dialectic, would suggest that the content of such terms would be determined by the historical, cultural, and social milieu of a particular epoch.

Further, there are implicit teleological overtones to such a claim, as it is only within a different age that one would be able to decipher the alienating features of a previous one. One does not assess the alienating features of the bourgeois era within its own paradigm. Liberalism does not assess itself from the perspective of the owning class, but as a repository of freedom. Only the imposition of a teleological project can force itself onto the present from a yet undetermined future. More will be said about that later.

So although there is only a very weak model of materialism suggested by the *1844 Manuscripts*, its normative components are very pronounced. Capitalism is characterized as an economic arrangement that is organized around human greed and avarice and is essentially a war among the avaricious.[25] In capitalism, money is viewed as the supreme good.[26] It is organized around swindle and plunder.[27] Everyone comes to view their neighbor's needs as something that can be exploited for their personal gain.[28]

In such a system those who labor are simply considered one more tool, a commodity to be consumed in the production process.[29] Industrial processes turn the workers into appendages of the machine, stripping the human being of their essence and denying them their species being.[30] The division of labor fragments the complete human being to extract a sliver of their essence as repetitive labor within the industrial process of production.[31]

It is impossible to read this and not be impressed by Marx's humanity and his commitment to the worth and well-being of the vast multitudes who toil for miniscule rewards. Such an analysis has been very influential in the humanistic schools of Marxist thought. It could be argued that this is actually the strongest basis from which Marx can launch his critique of capitalism.

However, the normative, humanistic, and essentialist claims are ultimately not the ones Marx wants to employ. He wants to identify historically valid empirical indicators in order to make causal statements about the direction of the social and political world. To do that it is necessary to look for indicators of capitalism's dysfunction in areas other than human essence.

The German Ideology

The epistemological model prevalent in Marx's time rests on a subject/object dichotomy. There is an observer who categorizes the sensations given by objects, and through this process the observer generates knowledge. For Marx such a model is disconnected from the reality of human existence. It suggests that consciousness and the content of human thought are autonomous phenomena, independent of life and the dynamic character of sensual contact with the world.

Marx's point can be seen in his comments on Hegel. In the unpublished fragment on Hegel's *Philosophy of Right*, Marx criticizes Hegel for suggesting that empirical reality has a rationality "outside of itself."[32] In discussing the rise of the state, Marx says of Hegel's notion, "Speculative philosophy expresses this fact as the ideas' deed, not as the idea of the multitude . . . "[33] Consciousness is divorced from existence. Material reality is a phenomenal manifestation of universal reason.

In the *German Ideology* the concern with Hegel still persists. Marx makes it clear that he rejects the Hegelian idealism and its view that somehow the world is a manifestation of the absolute. Of German philosophy, he says it moves from "heaven to earth."[34] The epistemological problem for Hegelian idealism is described in the *Holy Family*. In challenging the notion of causality presented by idealist, Herr Szeliga, Marx demonstrates the logical difficulty with Hegelian epistemology.

In what can only be described as a humorous passage ridiculing speculative philosophy Marx addresses the relationship between a particular entity, in this case apples, strawberries, pears, and almonds, and the general concept "fruit." The problem is in the relationship between the existence of the real object and the generalized concept used to describe a class of objects. To Marx, speculative philosophy has the orders of appearance reversed. It must assert the appearance of particular objects such as strawberries, apples, and so on as manifestations of the reality of "Absolute Fruit."[35] "Particular real fruits are no more than semblances whose true essence is 'the Substance'— 'Fruit.'"[36] The real emanates from the idea. To Marx, such a scheme is backwards.

The split with Hegel also encompasses the understanding of causality within politics. The Hegelian view of the state gives unity and purpose to the people residing within the whole of its organic union. In the state, the differences that manifest themselves as differences of interests and material struggles are surpassed in favor of a singular bond that binds citizens into a transcendent union. Marx rejected the mystical character of the union suggested by Hegel. Human beings do not transcend the barriers brought about by their material differences. They exist at the level of what Hegel terms "civil society." Civil society is the reality of human intercourse. It is, therefore, the real basis of human interaction upon which our understanding of history must rely.[37]

Marx is interested in material facts as his starting point, but not in the "dead facts" of empiricism.[38] He is interested in the explanation of our self-understanding of the world but wants material premises as the starting point for his analysis. In the *German Ideology*, much of that interest manifests itself in a discussion of consciousness.

The starting point for Marx's analysis is the existence of real individuals. However, their existence cannot be divorced from the activity that forms both the precondition for the material existence and the basis for the formation of their self-understanding of the world.[39] Living human beings are characterized by sensuous activity. Their connection to the world is through the senses and the ideas they form are a direct result of this activity.

Consciousness, as the formation of ideas about the world, cannot be divorced the activity performed by human beings in the world. Life is active, not passive. "Consciousness can never be anything else than conscious existence, and the existence of men is their action life-process."[40]

> The phantoms formed in the human brain are also, necessarily, sublimates of their material life-process, which is empirically verifiable and bound to material premises. Morality, religion, metaphysics, all the rest of ideology and their corresponding forms of consciousness thus no longer retain the semblance of independence. They have no history, no development; but men, developing their material production and their material intercourse, alter, along with this their real existence, their thinking and the products of their thinking. Life is not determined by consciousness, but consciousness by life.[41]

So the question is: how do we come to an understanding of who we are and how we have come to a particular position in history with all of the corresponding beliefs and practices? We cannot arrive at this understanding from pure thought or from teleological conceptions of metaphysics. Study must begin with the concrete existence of human beings. Further, there must be a material explanation of how they come to form an understanding of their conditions. This consciousness is shaped by their material activity in the world. For Marx, the primary material activity is production.

Production satisfies the needs of existence.[42] For that reason, it is an expression of life.[43] Therefore, production should be the starting point for any study of human beings and the conditions that have generated their ideas. Human beings distinguish themselves from other animals because they are able to engage in producing for their anticipated needs.

Production is central to the formation of human consciousness, but the conditions that shape consciousness are not the result of individual will or intentions. Production is a social and historical condition and is a reflection of stage material and technological development.[44] It is an objective, material condition that shapes the character of law, politics, religion, and social institutions. It does so by creating the ideas, or consciousness, that allow for the acceptance of particular practice.[45]

Hence there is an evolving notion of consciousness that has a central role in historical change. The sensuous contact with the world shapes the content of consciousness, which then serves as a gatekeeper for the ability of new ideas and practices to come into existence. Only when the material conditions are aligned with the ideological developments in the consciousness of human beings can history transform itself.

Ideas have material origins, but they also have material force. For Marx, the two cannot be separated. As he stated in the *Contribution to the Critique of Hegel's Philosophy of Right*, material force can only be overthrown by a material force. But, Marx continues, "theory itself becomes a material force when it has seized the masses."[46] When conditions have shaped the content of consciousness to the degree that social and political status quo is no longer consistent with the self-understanding of reality presented by consciousness, a revolutionary situation exists.

Material conditions give substance to consciousness. It is in the process of producing the condition for life that our ideas and attitudes are shaped. This consciousness represents our self-understanding of the world and our place within it. It is the totality of our understanding of the human condition.

The generation of consciousness is, therefore, a necessary condition for the construction of the superstructure, the social, political, and cultural institutions that spring from its base. However, these patterns of human association are the reflections of consciousness formed in the human mind. Therefore, they are the idealized manifestation of thought, shaped by the mode of production and turned into the material conditions in the superstructure for continued systemic reproduction. The formation of ideas is necessary for the construction of the superstructure.

In the *German Ideology* Marx makes clear that his method is to be distinguished from that of Kant and Hegel. He gives no independent status to consciousness. However, Marx has not abandoned the concerns regarding consciousness and its formation. Instead of an autonomous consciousness unfolding dialectically, Marx describes a material process that shapes the formation of human's self-understanding. The unfolding of a process in history still operates. The process still moves dialectically.

Thus, the direction taken by Marx in the *German Ideology* is one of creating a kind of materialist phenomenology in which a teleology of history stands in for Absolute Spirit. He is still under the influence of the master when it comes to assigning history a trajectory. How do human beings direct their intentional actions in the world? How is human experience transformed into the structures that shape the social order? If the Cartesian system has failed to account for life as activity, what alternative can be constructed that is dynamic?

The answers are found within a materialist reading of the *Phenomenology of the Spirit*. For Marx, consciousness needs to be given a material basis, one that is dynamic and transformative. The ideas that allow us to understand our historical conditions cannot be fixed and static. Each stage of material development generates a new self-understanding that overcomes the previous one.

Consciousness is at the core of all these transformations. Consciousness is formed out of the sensuous activity of human beings as they produce the material necessities of life. The evolving dynamic of history establishes the material basis for social evolution. Each new mode of production transforms human consciousness.

Self-awareness lies at the center of these concerns. A human being must be aware of the material processes that affect the formation of their ideas, beliefs, and actions. History passes through a series of ideological moments that are represented in the social and political institutions of the time. The institutions are transformed when the content of consciousness overturns.

While this could lead one to believe that Marx was a strict determinist, a more lenient interpretation of his notion of causality could also be employed. Described in a softer way, what Marx is outlining is a method of human identity formation. Human beings define themselves in relation to their experiences and the system of rewards and punishments available to them within the social order. It is a matter of psychological conditioning that channels the formation of consciousness in a particular direction. However, consciousness can overturn the existing order only when the historical conditions are ready for such a change.

Capital

To this point in the analysis of Marx's writings, the early work was examined and found to be largely normative in nature. In the *1844 Manuscripts*, greed and avarice established the causal dynamic for capitalist practice. This form of social practice was argued to contradict human essence. In the *German Ideology* Marx creates a materialist interpretation of consciousness tied to the historical forms of production. Sensuous activity forms consciousness, and consciousness provides the basis for the construction of human identity and the social practices within the relations of society.

Still, the articulation of central laws of history that would warrant Engels's comparison of Marx to Charles Darwin seems to be lacking. Darwin found specific evidence of evolutionary change. Drawing on the specifics of his observations aboard the *Beagle*, he generated inductively drawn hypotheses about the workings of evolution. His theory of "natural selection" followed the parameters of scientific syntax. Can Marx parallel that effort? The closest Marx comes is in the arguments found in *Capital* and other works of that period in Marx's writings. However, there is an important caveat.

Materialism and scientific analysis are clearly linked in the eyes of Marx and Engels. Therefore, the question as to the meaning of science cannot be divorced from the matter of materialist analysis. But is Marx engaging the scientific method outlined by Sir Francis Bacon and applied by people like Darwin? Yes, if by science one means the logical analysis of facts. However, the type of logic employed differs from what is normally meant by "science." Bacon and Darwin are engaging induction. Marx's analysis of capitalism is largely, although not exclusively, characterized by deduction. That is, the laws of capitalist practice, and the impact these practices have on workers, production, and the direction of capitalist activity, are largely contained within the definitional content of capitalism itself. This statement is not designed to diminish Marx's accomplishment. The work on capital is an extraordinary elaboration of capitalism's character. However, the explanation of its character is deduced from the internal logic of its practice. Marx's attempts at inductive hypotheses largely centers on the fate of capitalism, the historical inevitability of which is open to question.

It must also be stated that in analyzing these writings it is necessary to distinguish between the methodology and the content. This is the case because of the inability of materialist methods to stabilize concepts or decontextualize the origin of ideas. As was discussed in chapter 1, this leads to the relativized nature of all content used in historical analysis. For Marx, therefore, capitalism is a system-level dynamic that has historical origins that are linked to the mode of production in a given society. That means that capitalism must be approached as a set of activities that are bound to a particular historical epoch, and that all of the statements regarding capitalist developments must be understood as relative to that historical period. Not only are the practices of capitalism that Marx discusses bound to the period in which he is discussing them, but the analysis in which Marx is engaged must be understood as relative to the articulation of capitalist practice in his era. Again, this point is not intended to diminish Marx's work, but simply to state that all materialist analysis must contain a certain level of relativity and contextuality in order to maintain consistency.

While the issue of relativism is also relevant to the matter of methodology, the relativity of context would be governed by larger paradigmatic shifts in our understanding of the epistemological requirements of truth claims and the nature of scientific constructions. In the case of Marx, the paradigmatic shift had already occurred and the rules of scientific syntax were generally formed as he was developing his method. The point here being that according to Marx's own articulated assumptions, if we are looking for what is lasting in Marx's materialist analysis of history, it may be found more in the method than in the content. The methodological underpinnings of his logic may be of greater significance than each individual conclusion on the nature of the capitalism, as many of those conclusions may have greater relevance to his experience of the middle of the nineteenth century.

The scope of Marx's writings on capitalism makes it necessary to divide the work into several sections. This will include a discussion of the dynamics of capitalism, its effects on the working class, the laws and contradictions Marx identifies, and an analysis of the extent to which Marx's predictions and teleological statements disrupt his materialist efforts. Particular emphasis will be given to the causal "laws" that Marx identifies and the material nature of those claims.

The Workings of Materialist History

People are born into sets of relations, the content of which they did not design. This is true for both the owners and the workers of the capitalist system.

> In the social production of their existence, men inevitably enter into definite relations, which are independent of their will, namely relations of production appropriate to a given stage in the development of their material forces of production. The totality of these relations of production constitutes the economic structure of society, the real foundation, on which arises a legal and political superstructure and to which correspond definite forms of social consciousness. The mode of production of material life conditions the general process of social, political and intellectual life. It is not the consciousness of men that determines their existence, but their social existence that determines their consciousness.[47]

This is a materialist view of social and political transformation. The sensuous activity of human beings, engaged in the production of the necessities of existence, is manifested in idealized form in the institutional byproducts of those practices. The institutions then regulate human interaction.

In this materialist dynamic of history, it is the method of production that has a direct causal link to the institutional order that is manifest.

> The changes in the economic foundation lead sooner or later to the transformation of the whole immense superstructure. In studying such transformations it is always necessary to distinguish between the material transformation of the economic conditions of production, which can be determined with the precision of natural science, and the legal, political, religious, artistic or philosophic—in short, ideological forms in which men become conscious of the conflict and fight it out.[48]

The mode of production creates a consciousness within which social practices are generated. Marx calls the aggregate of these the "relations of production." So one of the causal laws that Marx identifies is that the mode of production determines the relations of production. This claim has led some to identify Marx as an economic determinist. However, when one is seeking laws of human behavior, it will always be necessary to engage is some reductionism in order to make statements of causality.

The Conditions of Labor

In *Capital*, Marx makes it clear that he wants to move away from the normative analysis that engaged so much of the *1844 Manuscripts*. His goal is to articulate the laws that operationalized the set of relations known as capitalism. What makes capitalism different than the feudal system that came before it is that while capitalism must produce goods that have "use-value," the systemic dynamic that drives it is production for "exchange-value." As Marx puts it, "In order to be able to extract value from the consumption of a commodity, our friend Moneybags, must be so lucky as to find, . . . a commodity, whose use-value possesses the peculiar property of being a source of value . . . "[49] Such a commodity is found in labor power. For that reason Marx characterized capitalism as a system in which there is the domination of past materialized labor, in the form of productive capital, over living labor.[50]

Much of *Capital*, and the analysis of capitalism more generally, can be described as a reorientation of the reader to an understanding of the effects of capitalism on the conditions of the working class. The liberal market economics found at the nexus of John Locke, Adam Smith, and Jeremy Bentham is a manifestation of the ideology of the owning class. Capitalism had advantages over feudalism, but the contradictions within the logic of capitalism are now beginning to manifest themselves requiring a new set of human relations.

Labor puts its "vital force" into the objects it produces.[51] However, the way in which capitalism is constructed, its economic logic, disconnects the value a worker generates from the amount that the worker receives in compensation. Wages are set by the supply and demand for workers in the marketplace.[52] This means that any force that influences the availability of workers for production will influence the amount they are paid and, hence, their well-being.

This system of compensation for the workers leads to the creation of what Marx calls "surplus value." Put simply, surplus value is profit. It is created when the sale of products exceeds the cost of production.[53] The term is used to indicate that the "surplus" is the value extracted from the workers beyond that for which they are compensated. Capitalists claim the right to surplus value as they brought the labor power and raw materials together in the production process.[54] The worker has only his or her labor time to sell and this takes place in a competitive environment with other workers engaged in the same process.

In that sense, both owners and workers operate in a market environment. However, two points need to be stressed. Even though there is competition in both realities, the experiences that owners and workers have are fundamentally different, so much so that the consciousness formed through the sensual contact with the world leads to two different and conflictual forms of consciousness. Second, the creation of liberal ideology was a historical product tied to the rise of small-scale production and the rise of a diverse owning class. It needs to be viewed as both a historical and a social product, subject to the alteration of conditions that have served as its formation.

Historical Laws and Contradictions of Capitalism

Materialism is not synonymous with class analysis. It is more correctly considered an epistemological and ontological claim. Therefore, it is not the plight of the workers within capitalism that gives historical materialism its materialist pedigree, but the fact that Marx identifies causal connections and historical contradictions that are significant to the movement of history.

The notion of a dialectical process of historical change suggests that at specific periods in history the internal contradictions inherent in all system-level dynamics will manifest themselves and produce a transformation of conditions and practices. Capitalism is certainly no exception. The question of whether or not the contradictions in capitalism serve as a demonstration sufficient to prove the validity of historical dialectics is not the interest here. The question is one of causal sufficiency within a materialist understanding of history.

Has Marx identified enough dynamic processes internal to capitalism to warrant the label materialist? That is, are there material forces that have been identified sufficient to cause the movement of history? The answer is yes. However, it cannot be said without qualification. Most of the causal dynamics and contradictions identified are tied to two conditions of capitalism: the tendency of capitalism to create monopolies and the plight of labor under the conditions of capitalism. The role of production in determining all system-level dynamics throughout history is simply afforded too scant attention to justify the claim that Marx has demonstrated the exclusive causal role of production for all major historical changes. The mention of the historical role of production in both the *Manifesto* and the *Critique of Political Economy* is not sufficient to demonstrate such a sweeping causal statement.

However, within capitalism the explanatory power of Marx's materialist critique is difficult to deny. The logic of capitalism traps both owners and workers in systems in which not only must surplus value be extracted from the workers but the extraction must be maximized. This is the case because part of that value is reinvested in machines that increase the productivity of labor. Productivity must be maximized or the owners will find themselves losing market share and ultimately their business will close. Machines are used to increase surplus value.[55] The division of labor is used to increase surplus value.[56] These increases could be used to shorten the workday, but this cannot occur as long as capitalist competition dominates the economic landscape.

For this reason, the amount of capital employed in production must continually increase. The use of machinery, women, children, and the division of labor will all be employed to drive down labor costs as they make the value of individual labor decline. Machines will be used to replace laborers in the factories. It is the nature of capitalism to move toward ever cheaper means of production.[57]

Marx makes it clear that there is a floor below which the wages of the workforce cannot fall. As a system, workers must have enough to survive and reproduce the workforce for succeeding generations. However, the continual downward pressure on wages is actually a byproduct of the increasing productivity of labor.

> The law by which a constantly increasing quantity of means of production, thanks to the advance in the productiveness of social labor, may be set in movement by a progressively diminishing expenditure of human power, this law, in a capitalist society—where the laborer does not employ the means of production, but the means of production employ the laborer—undergoes a complete inversion and is expressed thus: the higher the productiveness of labor the greater is the pressure of the laborers on the means of employment, the more precarious, therefore, becomes their condition of existence . . .[58]

All the methods of increasing the productivity of labor are carried out at the expense of the laborer and for the benefit of the owning class.

Owners that do not maximize the productivity of labor and minimize their expenditures for labor power will find themselves losing out to those who do. Thus, it is the tendency of capital to concentrate with the development of the means of production.[59] This situation is enhanced by the economy of scale in production.

> The battle of competition is carried on by the cheapening of commodities. Other things being equal, the cheapness of commodities depends on the productivity of labor, which, in turn, depends upon the scale of production. Large capitals, therefore, get the better of small ones.[60]

Capitalists must expand production capacity in order to compete. The resources necessary to expand come from the value they can extract from the workforce. The result will be the concentration of capital in fewer and fewer hands and a growing class of unemployed, underemployed, and impoverished workers.

An economic system that is dependent on expanding markets and expanding consumption cannot be sustained without a population that has sufficient purchasing power to consume the products being produced. However, with capitalism, the constant need to reduce production costs, and the requirement that labor be considered as a component of cost, means that value afforded to labor to sustain itself will be pushed to subsistence levels. This will result in insufficient demand for the goods generated by industrial production. Such a dynamic generates system-level instability.

The Normative and the Scientific

Much of the analysis of capitalism is focused on identifying its internal dynamics. Marx is attempting to demonstrate that there are laws that govern the operation of capitalism. Marx is also arguing that some of the dynamics within capitalism produce outright contradictions when followed to their logical conclusions. The analysis is complex, detailed, and extraordinary in its depth and clarity.

However, projecting an analysis of the present onto the future is always a dangerous task. Marx clearly identifies logical, material processes that operate within capitalism. However, when Marx projects the analysis of capitalism onto the larger frame of history to make statements he regards as "causally necessary" developments in the future of human history, the analysis begins to move away from material analysis and is muddled by his commitments to social justice for the working class and the desire for revolutionary change.[61]

Such claims move Marx away from pure materialism. The working class must inevitably come to power.[62] The proletariat must become the ruling class.[63] The working class is the multitude. Democracy demands their rule. Workers are also the class that adds their "vital force" to the production process, giving them an historical status as the class most connected to the reality generated by human productive activity.

However, at this stage in his analysis Marx has left the scientific analysis behind in favor of a political commitment to an economic class that he views as exploited. These are arguments in favor of why the working class *should* rule, not that its rule is *inevitable*. To paraphrase Hume, Marx has moved from "is" to "ought" and departed from a materialist analysis.

Marx has not transcended ideological commitments in favor of historical laws, but has generated an alternative ideological narrative to that of the bourgeois order. In this narrative, there is to be no distinction between intellectual work and physical labor. The real questions of the distribution of labor have to do with the distribution of "labor time." The saving of labor time is the measure of social progress.[64] In the end, justice will be determined by each giving what they can and taking what they need.

These claims are indeed revolutionary, but they are part of a normative framework that is an alternative to that found in bourgeois society. They cannot be found in history because history can possess no values. The materiality of such claims, that they maintain an objective standing outside of the contextual conditions that gave rise to them, is problematic. That is not to say that such claims are good or bad, simply that they represent an ideological position that has its origins in a specific set of historical conditions and do not represent ahistorical truths.

Marx has left the discussion of causality behind and substituted his political commitment to a class he sees as oppressed and in doing so has asserted a normative claim into the discussion. Capitalism does produce a complex and systematic extraction of value out of the working class. The processes of capitalist production do produce downward pressure on wages and a logic for minimal redistributive actions on the part of governmental institutions. That argument is causal and material. However, the case for working class rule is essentialist and normative.

MARX AND MATERIALISM

In assessing the materialist character of Marx's writing it is necessary to return to the model of materialism outlined in chapter 1. As was stated, no figure in the field of social and political thought is a perfect materialist. It is impossible to escape the metaphysical character of language, as language is used to represent, even when used to critique the process of representation. Still, it is important to assess the strengths and weaknesses of the various types of materialism in order to gauge their contribution to a materialist understanding of the social world.

Marx makes it clear he rejects the idea of transcendental truth claims. Our understanding of the world is carried out through the interaction of the human being with the totality of economic, social, and cultural forces to which they are exposed. Ideas, ideologies, and consciousness are shaped by that connection to the material conditions of experience.

Less clear is whether or not there is a full rejection of all universalist claims regarding human subjectivity, even when arrived at through a material analysis of history. Even when language less overt than the essentialism of the *1844 Manuscripts* is employed, there are still shadows of the harder ontological claims regarding human essence, moral imperatives, and the teleology of history. Marx's interpreters are still discussing whether the path of history will provide the liberation of the working class or whether the values of democracy and justice will need a rebirth in order to end human oppression. Such seeming contradictions are discussed by Steven Lukes in *Marxism and Morality*.[65] Even though Lukes favors a more humanistic reading of Marx, his work demonstrates the problem of trying to clarify Marx's position.

More clear, in my view, is the position Marx adopts with regard to the significance of life as animated activity. Life is action. Life involves sensuous contact with the world and through that process ideas are formed. This explains why Marx rejected what he saw as the dead materialism of empiricism in favor of placing the materiality of life at the core of his analysis. Marx's position leads authors such as Pheng Cheah to conclude that Marx's project contains "an ontology of organismic vitalism."[66] Such a claim is based on the significance of living being as an intermediary between the material reality and the formation of consciousness. While Cheah makes an interesting point, the term "vitalism" conjures up such metaphysical baggage that another term might be more useful.

For this reason, the work of the *German Ideology* is so important. Marx is trying to incorporate both the ongoing dynamics of lived experience with the formations of ideas and consciousness that can serve as both the motivators and directors of human activity. Consciousness mediates between direct sensation and action. These ideas, held in the minds of human beings, can transform the course of history. Historical conditions are, therefore, not the direct origins of social change, but the source and initiator for the formation of consciousness which then directs of the course of history.

When it comes to human nature, many, if not most, of Marx's comments reflect a historically and contextually constructed view of human nature. This is less the case in the *1844 Manuscripts*, but since there are legitimate questions about how Marx viewed the *Manuscripts* their worth can be discounted within the overall assessment. Particularly in the *German Ideology*, subjectivity is argued to be a complex construction out of the economic, social, and political forces found in the culture. It is the role those conditions play in the formation of identity, subjectivity, and ideology that is the key to understanding the revolutionary potential of Marx's analysis. Consciousness, and its political corollary, ideology, is continually transformed though the sensual contact of the individual with the historical conditions found in the environment and the ideological constructions that constitute the social and political milieu of a given age. These experiences are incorporated into the individual's consciousness where they acquire their meaning and motivational potential.

Therefore, the separation of base and superstructure in Marx's analysis is problematic to this understanding. The separation of base and superstructure, with the claim that the productive base is the cause of all the practices found in the superstructure, is overly deterministic and would negate the independence and variety of social processes that could influence the evolution of ideological formations, institutional change, and the varying rates at which they may transform. If ideas may have material force, then ideas may influence the formation of other ideas, causing the base/superstructure model to break down. Moving away from this formula allows for analysis to include a broader set of potential influences characterizing the ideological formations of a particular historical epoch.

On the positive side, Marx provides a good primer for understanding materiality of political power. "The ruling ideas of each age have ever been the ideas of its ruling class."[67] Religion, philosophy, and the cultural norms of the social order are taught and socialized into the public in a manner consistent with the maintenance of the ruling class. This provides a legitimizing feedback loop for the exercise of raw power. This means that political prescriptions have their origins in the interests found in society rather than the articulation and implementation of universal truths.

Finally, there is the question of where this analysis is intended to go. Marx indicates that the pursuit of private utility is terminated with the overthrow of rule by the bourgeoisie. When the proletariat develops a new consciousness they will throw off their chains and participate in the democracy that solves the riddle of political history. Freedom is found within the community.

But how close does such a political gesture place him to the Hegelian description of the state? Liberal capitalism is asserted to be the last antagonistic form of political association. Communism transcends the struggle over private property. Is the Hegelian state, the organic union of all of societal activities, achieved in a communist society? Is such a union Marx's ultimate objective? From what source does freedom emerge in a teleology of human history?

What does this say about the historical nature of truth, one of the conditions of materialism outlined in chapter 1? It means that even with his outline of the dialectics of change and the transformative nature of revolutionary upheaval, that rather than purely historicizing truth, Marx is seeking to provide an alternative to bourgeois truth. He has not fully relativized truth construction, which means not fully materialized its processes. The same can be said of his normative position. He has not relativized ethics but has instead provided an alternative ethics to the liberal model founded on private property and private accumulation.

CONCLUSION

In *Specters of Marx*, Jacques Derrida discusses the debt that is owed to Marx. Marx sets the stage for the further development of materialist philosophy as he provides a critical analysis of the metaphysics and essentialist ontologies that have dominated Western social science. Derrida's own methodological approach, deconstruction, would not be possible in a pre-Marxian environ-

ment of social inquiry. It is only in the aftermath of Marx's critical materialism that the questions surrounding metaphysical methods, the imposition of
logocentrism, the ideological character of consciousness, and hegemony of
language could be addressed.[68]

Marx represents a major step in the development of materialist social
science, but he is a beginning and not an end. As Derrida puts it in a work
entitled *Positions*, "Now, we cannot consider Marx's, Engels's, or Lenin's
texts as completely finished elaborations that are simply to be 'applied' to the
current situations. In saying this, I am not advocating anything contrary to
'Marxism.' I am convinced of it."[69]

But that is not to suggest total agreement. Marx is too close to the Hegelian system for that. Derrida is not a dialectician. Nevertheless, the spirit of
critical inquiry owes a debt to the Marxian system.

Another admiring critic of Marx's analysis was Max Weber. Weber
called Marx's work "brilliant" and insightful. Still, he was critical of elements in the Marxian project. Weber was developing his own model of
materialist analysis, one that was focused on the empirically verifiable events
of history, but within a neo-Kantian framework of causality. Weber's analysis subsumed the entire Marxian system under his methodology. Whether it
constitutes a step forward or backward is open to interpretation. However, its
power and influence in the twentieth century cannot be denied. It is to that
system that we will now turn.

NOTES

1. Friedrich Engels, "Speech at the Graveside of Karl Marx," in *The Marx-Engels Reader*, edited by Robert Tucker, (New York: Norton, 1978), 681.
2. G. W. F. Hegel, *Phenomenology of the Mind* (New York: Harper and Row, 1967), 131.
3. Hegel, *The Phenomenology of the Mind*, 133.
4. G. W. F. Hegel, *The Philosophy of History* (New York: Dover, 1956), 17.
5. Hegel, *The Philosophy of History*, 16.
6. Hegel, *The Philosophy of History*, 78
7. Ludwig Feuerbach, "Principles of the Philosophy of the Future," in *The Fiery Brook: Selected Writings of Ludwig Feuerbach* (Garden City, NY: Doubleday and Company, 1972), 178.
8. Feuerbach, 182.
9. Feuerbach, 177.
10. Feuerbach, 179.
11. Feuerbach, 200.
12. Karl Marx, "Theses on Feuerbach." in *The Marx-Engels Reader*, 143.
13. Marx, "Theses on Feuerbach," 144.
14. Karl Marx, "Economic and Philosophic Manuscripts of 1844," in *The Marx-Engels Reader*, 86.
15. Marx, "1844 Manuscripts," 71.
16. Marx, "1844 Manuscripts," 71.
17. Marx, "1844 Manuscripts," 71.
18. Marx, "1844 Manuscripts," 74.
19. Marx, "1844 Manuscripts," 74.

20. Marx, "1844 Manuscripts," 76.
21. Marx, "1844 Manuscripts," 78.
22. Marx, "1844 Manuscripts," 101.
23. Marx, "1844 Manuscripts," 85, 89.
24. Marx, "1844 Manuscripts," 75, 76.
25. Marx, "1844 Manuscripts," 71.
26. Marx, "1844 Manuscripts," 103.
27. Marx, "1844 Manuscripts," 93.
28. Marx, "1844 Manuscripts," 94.
29. Marx, "1844 Manuscripts," 70.
30. Marx, "1844 Manuscripts," 95.
31. Marx, "1844 Manuscripts," 95.
32. Marx, "Contribution to the Critique of Hegel's Philosophy of Right," in *The Marx-Engels Reader*, 17.
33. Marx, "Contribution to the Critique of Hegel's Philosophy of Right," 17.
34. Marx, "The German Ideology," in *The Marx-Engels Reader*, 154
35. Karl Marx, "The Holy Family," in *Karl Marx: Selected Writings*, edited by David McLellan (Oxford, UK: Oxford University Press, 1985), 137.
36. Marx, "Holy Family," 136.
37. Marx, "German Ideology," 163.
38. Marx, "German Ideology," 155.
39. Marx, "German Ideology," 149, 154.
40. Marx, "German Ideology," 154.
41. Marx, "German Ideology," 154-155.
42. Marx, "German Ideology," 156.
43. Marx, "German Ideology," 150.
44. Marx, "German Ideology," 154.
45. Marx, "German Ideology," 165.
46. Marx, "Contribution to the Critique of Hegel's Philosophy or Right," 60.
47. Karl Marx, *A Contribution to the Critique of Political Economy*, edited by Maurice Dobb (New York: International Publishers, 1970), 20-21.
48. Marx, *Critique of Political Economy*, 21.
49. Marx, "Capital," in *The Marx-Engels Reader*, 336.
50. Marx, "Wage Labor and Capital, in *The Marx-Engels Reader*, 209
51. Marx, "Capital," 354.
52. Marx, "Wage Labor and Capital," 206.
53. Marx, "Capital," 358.
54. Marx, "Capital," 357.
55. Marx, "Capital," 403.
56. Marx, "Capital," 400.
57. Marx, "Wage Labor and Capital," 214.
58. Marx, "Capital," 430.
59. Marx, "Capital," 437.
60. Karl Marx, *Capital*, (New York: Dutton Publishing, 1974), 691.
61. That is not to suggest that social justice is not a worthy value. It is only to suggest that social justice is a "value" and therefore lends itself less to the material analysis of history.
62. Marx, "Capital," in *The Marx-Engels Reader*, 414.
63. Marx, "The Communist Manifesto," in *The Marx-Engels Reader*, 490.
64. For a discussion of the role played by "time" in Marx's analysis see the later chapters of the *Grundrisse*.
65. Steven Lukes, *Marxism and Morality* (Oxford, UK: Oxford University Press, 1987).
66. Cheah, Pheng. "Non-Dialectical Materialism," in *New Materialisms*, edited by Diana Coole and Samantha Frost (Durham, NC: Duke University Press, 2010), 71.
67. Marx, "The Communist Manifesto," 489.
68. Jacques Derrida, *Specters of Marx* (New York: Routledge, 1994), 92.
69. Jacques Derrida, *Positions* (Chicago: University of Chicago Press, 1981), 63.

Chapter Four

Weber

Materialism and Methodology

INTRODUCTION

There are few figures as important as Max Weber in the development of twentieth-century social science. While Weber is not often discussed in the context of furthering a materialist understanding of the world he is actually a very important figure in its development. As I have suggested elsewhere,[1] Weber's assertion regarding the role and subjective components of human values was significant in the development of twentieth-century philosophy and social science methodology. It also conveys one piece of the relativism that I argue is a central component of materialist philosophy.

It is important to note that Weber always asserted that social science should be made as scientific as possible and should always rely on empirical reference points as it establishes causal hypotheses about the developments in history. He was not interested in metaphysical explanations of cultural and historical change, and openly challenges his readers to leave the religiosity of the past behind.[2]

To Weber, the social scientist is interested in micro-causality. The investigator wants to know what is causally significant for the occurrence of particular events in history. This means that he rejected both dialectical and historicist methodologies as overly vague and general. Instead Weber offers his own system, interpretive sociology. Interpretive sociology seeks specific answers to specific questions of historical change. He rejects the idea that there are overarching laws of historical development. He sees such claims as heuristic devices with little value as social science.

Weber's methodological system operationalizes and magnifies some of the materialist elements found in the Kantian system. It expands the suspicions of metaphysis outlined in *The Critique of Pure Reason* and eliminates metaphysics from the discussion of causality. It transforms the Kantian notion of infinite causal threads in history and addresses them as an empirical problem to be addressed by the social sciences. Finally, Weber clearly saw himself and the method he created as constituting a break with the past. One must look forward and that is only accomplished with a materialist understanding of the world.

Does this make Weber the perfect materialist? Such a claim cannot be made. The neo-Kantian system that Weber develops is still heavily influenced by the Kantian ontology. It has static, essentialist elements regarding the structure and content of human subjectivity. It also fails to fully relativize the system of knowledge it relies on for its constructions. Nevertheless, Weber's significance in moving social inquiry in a materialist direction is undeniable.

THE CRITIQUE OF MARX

A good place to start developing Weber's position is to examine his critique of Marx. Weber's criticism of Marx is important for several reasons. First, some of Weber's points are important on their merits. There are legitimate questions surrounding the extent of Marx's break with Hegelian historicism and the teleology of history. Are the claims to "economic determinism" warranted? Is there a reformulation that can take place to quell the concerns?

Another reason that the contrast between Marx and Weber is important is that it provides a contrast between two fundamentally different methods, both of which seek to be as materialistic as they see possible. Can Weber somehow overcome the shortcomings in Marx's materialism and vice versa? Both methods were immensely important in the twentieth century and seen as, largely, mutually exclusive.

Finally, it is important to note some of Weber's criticisms of Marx because Weber identifies problems with which some of those sympathetic to the Marxian system will have to address. Louis Althusser, Jean Baudrillard, and Jacque Derrida all deal in some way with the issues that are originally raised by Weber, even though they are all sympathetic to Marx's project. This is particularly true with regard to the issues of class, economic reductionism, and the dialectic as a description of historical change. (These issues will be addressed in a later chapter.)

Max Weber's critique of Karl Marx's methodology proceeds from a simple assumption. Even though Marx was critical of Hegelian idealism, Marx was still very much a Hegelian in his method. This is the essence of Weber's methodological critique of Marx. To put it simply, Weber saw Marx as someone who put the Hegelian ontology "right side up," but nevertheless maintained the basic historicist methodology. Therefore, while Marx avoids the problems of the Hegelian universal subject, to Weber Marx is still engaging a basic historicist methodology.

Weber concluded that Hegel and Marx take as their point of departure the goal of defining general laws which govern historic change. This takes place using a teleological conception of history. Knowing the end of the historic process, and the causal determinants operating within human history, provides a seemingly powerful method for social analysis. A critique of the existing social order can proceed outside of any normative world view because the law of historic causality is combined with a historically accurate, non-subjective, "end" of social development. Weber questions the epistemological status of this method of historical and social analysis.

Weber also criticized the Hegelian tradition for trying to close the gap between concepts and reality by simply equating concepts with reality.[3] Within historicism, the concept is given a metaphysical status.[4] Weber was critical of the historicist Wilhelm Roscher precisely on this issue. Roscher's tendency was to treat a concept like "Volk" as a biologic entity and grant it properties such as evolution.[5] Weber was opposed to this position on the status of concepts, regarding them as the constructions of investigators.

According to Weber the result of the historicist's methodological perspective is that the concept, which is to be used as a tool in social research, has acquired the property of causality. The historicists then proceeds to search for the concepts that, in causal terms, can reproduce reality.[6] This requires that the final, all-inclusive, concept be discovered. Weber asserted that the historicists then propose to deduce reality from the generalized concept that they have created.[7] Weber argued that this is the method that Marx used in his analysis of history.

In Marxism, as in Hegelianism, the critique still emanates deductively from the teleology. Thus, Weber saw his criticism of historicism, that it tries to deduce reality from final abstract laws,[8] as also applicable to Marx's analysis. Once the abstract law is found, which to Marx was the tendency toward the dissolution of all barriers to humanity's productive potential, then the critique of existing social order takes place in relation to that abstract teleology. According to the Weberian perspective, the Marxist methodology tries to explain reality from this theoretical abstraction.

To Weber, no final abstract law has complete explanatory power. A concrete situation in history can never be deduced from abstract laws.[9] Laws and concepts only have heuristic value in historical analysis.[10]

From Weber's point of view there are two modes of analysis taking place simultaneously within the Marxian discussion of history. First of all, there is a "law" of historic development presented as a fact in the evolution of the human species. History has progressed in a specific direction. History moves toward the ever-increasing productivity of labor, as the mode of production becomes more organized and mechanized. Using concrete historical examples, Marx showed how the production process breaks down all barriers to its increased development. Eventually, capitalism will become a hindrance to this historical movement. It will fall as changes in the mode of production necessitate changes in the relations of production.

In Marx's analysis, however, there is a second and equally forceful argument regarding the "appropriateness" of capitalism for a truly human existence. Capitalism oppresses the majority of the population. It forces workers into wage slavery, denying them their truly creative powers and their freedom. To Weber's neo-Kantian world view, the issue of capitalism's "appropriateness" involves a value commitment.

From Weber's methodological perspective, Marx intertwines these two types of analysis.

Marx simultaneously presents us with a set of historical facts about the development of the means of production and a value judgment about the appropriateness of capitalism for a truly human existence. The Weberian methodology raises questions about the relationship between these two spheres of analysis. What, specifically, is the relationship between the statement of historical fact and the value positions espoused in Marx's writings? This relationship is fundamental to the distinction between the methodologies of Marx and Weber. Weber saw Marx as selectively interpreting history from a specific point of view. To Weber, only human beings can hold values, not history. History does not contain a teleology, but has a teleology imposed on it by individuals who interpret historical events.

The enterprise Marx undertook was an interpretation of selected historical facts based on his own values. Historical events were selected and placed into a conceptual framework of study because they reinforced the thesis that changes in the mode of production had a direct causal link to the social and political transformations that societies undergo.

Thus, to Weber, Marx selected historical events for their consistency with his own world view. To Weber, this confuses the relationship between facts and values. Historical facts can never yield values. Values are taken into study by the individual involved in historical research. Thus to Weber, Marx's teleology is nothing more than an exposition of Marx's own value system and world view and does not constitute the status of historical fact. Marx's analysis constitutes an objectification of his own subjective value position through the selected interpretation of history.

For that reason, Weber claimed that Marx was constructing a model for social and historical analysis, not generating iron-clad laws of historical development. Weber called these models "ideal-types," or pure conceptual schemes for the analysis of historical trends and social phenomena. An ideal-type is a tool for analysis, a framework for the orientation of empirical inquiry. It cannot produce "laws" as its outcome. Thus, claimed Weber, the "laws of history" asserted by Marx are actually ideal types. [11]

An ideal type is a conceptual pattern imposed on events by an investigator in order to promote understanding. [12]

> An ideal type is formed by the one-sided accentuation of one or more points of view and by the synthesis of a great many . . . concrete individual phenomena, which are arranged according to those one-sidedly emphasized viewpoints into a unified analytical construct. [13]

In itself, an ideal type does not represent reality, but offers only one possible way of interpreting reality. When Marx claims that "empirical observation must bring out the connection between the social and political structure and the mode of production," [14] he is expressing a commitment to one particular causal thread between human beings and society.

Weber admits that this one-sided accentuation of reality is precisely how social science proceeds. It cannot be otherwise. Human beings live inside an infinitely rich web of causality. They must choose among all the possible stimuli in order to make sense of it. However, the complete focus on economic causes is too narrow for Weber's conception of social explanation. The explanation of anything by purely economic causes, said Weber, is never exhaustive, even in economics. [15]

If Marx abandoned the concern for a "law" of historic development and its teleology, and if the materialist conception of history can be expressed as an ideal-typical interpretation of historical events, then Marxism contains its element of truth within the Weberian scheme. However, this truth stems from the fact that Marx imposed his value structure onto the analysis, not because history somehow conveyed a universal ethical standard that involves the liberation of the working class.

The commitment to a value determines the interest and the path of any investigation. This is recognized by Weber as a process which occurs in social scientific analysis. What is important to investigate is determined by the values of the investigator. [16] To Weber, this is precisely the activity in which Marx was engaged in his analysis of history.

NEO-KANTIANISM AND THE LIMITS OF KNOWLEDGE

Weber tried to make social science as materialistic as possible. However, this had to be accomplished within the confines of the Kantian epistemology under which he worked. As Weber put it, "the fundamental ideas of modern epistemology . . . ultimately derive from Kant . . . " [17] In the Kantian system, the investigator confronts an external reality, regardless of whether that reality is strictly physical or social, as an object foreign and separate from itself.

It is impossible to understand the Weberian model without appreciating its legacy from Kant. Kant describes material reality as part of an infinitely rich causal web. The mind is not infinite in its capacities, nor in its abilities to convey the infinite through communications. For Kant, this asserts that we only can know the "appearances" of objects, not their essence. For Weber, this means that in the social world the best we can hope for is "understanding" (Verstehen) of the social causality around us. Universal laws of history are beyond the scope of human inquiry.

The Kantian system is built on the notion of a distinction between the empirical world and the realm of intelligibility.[18] Human beings come to know the empirical world through the interaction of the senses with the activities of the mind. However, the mind is restricted in its capacity to grasp empirical reality due to the limited nature of the mechanisms employed. The five senses coupled with the categories of experience found in the mind can never convey the complexity of any object's true nature. We, therefore, never know an objective reality, only the appearance of reality.[19]

If this is true of the sense impressions left from contact with a concrete physical reality, the problem is compounded when Weber applies these ideas to social reality. Every event in the social world also has a complex nature which the human mind is incapable of grasping in its entirety. " . . . [A] description of even the smallest slice of reality can never be exhaustive. . . "[20] With the parameters of social knowledge thus restricted, the problem becomes one of defining a method that will make any aspect of the social world intelligible.

Weber's acceptance of the Kantian dualism shaped the methodological strategy employed in the study of social reality. The mind may have material premises, but the activities of the mind are unique to it realm. The reasoning mind confronts reality as an object alien to itself. In the study of society, as in the study of physical objects, events are never understood in their entirety. The mind is not capable of grasping the totality of history. Therefore, the social world requires interpretation.

THE METHOD OF INTERPRETATION

Weber summed up the Kantian approach to epistemology as follows: "Kant took for his point of departure the presupposition: 'Scientific proof exists and it is valid,' and then asked, 'Under which presuppositions of thought is truth possible and meaningful?'"[21] Of Weber, a similar statement regarding social scientific knowledge can be offered. Weber asked, "Given the essential separation of intellect and matter, and given the inherent limitations of the mind to grasp the material and social events of external experience in their entirety, what type of knowledge is possible?"

To Kant knowledge of the physical world was limited by the necessary interaction of subject and object. Sensation must be turned into cognition. To Weber, knowledge of the social environment is of a limited nature as well. His conclusion is simple. We never have a complete explanation of any historical or cultural phenomenon given the infinite causal complexity of each and every event in the world.

Weber responds to this condition by asserting that all social events require human interpretation. The actual occurrence of an event in history can be objectively stated. The complex of causes leading to the event requires that *significant* causal factors be identified within the infinite richness of the world. However, the assertion of *significance* has a subjective component. In fact, according to Weber, even the selection of a subject for historical study has a subjective element, as it must be considered important or meaningful to the investigator engaged in the study.

Weber sought to define a methodology that would make the social sciences as scientific as possible, but Weber was not a positivist. He states in *The Methodology of the Social Sciences* that value judgments are not the subject of causal analysis.[22] However, the interaction of facts and values in the human personality cannot be fully separated from the conduct of social research. What is to be studied, and the indicators of that study, engages the subjective, evaluative ideas of the investigator.[23] Values influence the topic of study and the indicators to be used in the analysis of causality. This is particularly true in the construction of the analytic tools of study, the ideal-type. It also leads Weber to conclusions about the subjective nature of social science validity.

What Weber, and the other neo-Kantians, suggested is that the mind, with its limited capacities, must confront the social environment as an object in the process of seeking to make it intelligible. This is the role played by the ideal-type. The ideal-type is a mental construct, a product of human intuition and cognition. It should never be mistaken for reality itself.[24] Borrowing the notion from Johann Gottfried Herder, Weber's ideal type is an intellectually pure concept created by an investigator to which empirical reality can be compared.[25] With conceptual purity, any deviation from the logically expected condition can be explained with reference to material circumstances of history.[26]

The ideal-type is particularly useful in the explanation of behavior carried out by groups of individuals. To Weber, concept such as "capitalism" and "bureaucracy" are ideal-types because these terms represent specific sets of substantive conditions and patterns of behavior but cannot be found in pure form in our social reality. Capitalism and bureaucracy are not tangible objects, but represent a collection of activities carried out by discrete individual actors. Deviations from behavior predicted by the model can be the basis for investigation.

However, the method of investigation cannot be carried out in the same way as in the natural sciences. Because social science relies so much on subjective factors and interpretation on the part of the investigator, the criteria for causal sufficiency differs greatly. In the natural sciences matters of causality can be measured and tested. In the realm of social and historical explanation, "[t]he historian's sense of the situation, his intuition uncover[s] causal interconnections. . . . The contrast with the natural sciences consists indeed precisely in the fact that the historian deals with the explanation of events and personalities which are 'interpreted' and 'understood' by direct analogy with our own intellectual, spiritual and psychological constitutions."[27] Causal hypotheses in the social sciences must conform with a common sense notion of causal sufficiency.[28]

What is striking about Weber's analysis is where he goes next. The validity of the historian's analysis is actually measured both socially and empirically. The analysis must conform to and engage with the empirical facts of history. Weber makes it very clear that the empirical facts are subject to verification as they must conform to the events of the historical record. However, the facts are also selected and organized by the investigator. Therefore, history is always an interpretation. That means that in the study of historical and cultural phenomena there is also participation from the engaged reader. "In the historical treatise it is . . . the suggestive vividness of its account report which allows the reader to 'empathize' with what has been depicted in the same way as that in which it is experienced and concretely grasped by the historian's own intuition . . . "[29] The historical must engage with the reader in order to complete the circle, the transmission of historical interpretation to another human being. For this reason, the great historians must have intuitive and artistic "gifts" in order to convey historical understanding. Historians who cannot connect with their readers will not have sway in the telling of history.

As is the case with the notion of charismatic domination, the connection between the actor and the follower is crucial. The telling of history is a social activity. It must replicate notions of causality and significance that are more widely shared in order to be considered historically valid.

In general, Weber has not separated himself from the transcendental elements of Kantian rationalism. Weber sees our reality as part of an infinitely complex causal web which must be interpreted by the finite beings seeking to make sense of it. The mind possesses creativity and intuition in constructing its interpretations.

But the activity of constructing knowledge is strictly carried out by investigators interpreting the historical data. There is no assertion of a law of history or a teleological undercurrent to human action. What must be interpreted is the material nature of causality as it relates to human social and cultural activity. In that sense, Weber has created a very human-centric method for the study of human activity, even as he places limits on the scope and the means of knowledge construction.

Methodological Individualism and Subjective Nature of Experience

Social science is the interpretive study of individuals in a social context. Social actions are defined as those actions which are affected by the existence and behavior of others.[30] But as with the creative process of intuition, only individuals have experiences and motives. Only individuals perform actions. Social science finds it useful to employ collective concepts in explaining action, but "collectivities must be treated as solely the resultants and modes of organization of the particular acts of individual persons, since these alone can be treated as agents in a course of subjectively understandable action."[31]

Weber's goal in social scientific research is, therefore, to understand the subjectively meaningful motives and goals of individuals acting in a social context. "Laws" of historic and social change can never convey the uniqueness of subjective meaning, nor the richness of historic events. "Laws" are not the goals of Weber's sociology, as they must be so general in character that they cannot contain significant content.[32] The complexity of an historical event is never conveyed by the search for regularity, but only in the explanation of its unique character.

There is another aspect to this rejection of "laws" as the goals of Weber's analysis. The search for laws in the explanation of human behavior implies that there exists an objective level at which analysis can occur outside of a subjective orientation on the part of the investigator and the subject. Weber rejects this idea.

The search for some objective totality is outside the parameters of human understanding. The individual is not able to grasp the infinite complexity of social and historic reality. Subjective interpretation is therefore necessary. The subjectivity of the human experience is clearly portrayed in Weber's description of culture. "Culture is a finite segment of the meaningless infinity of the world process, a segment on which human beings confer meaning and significance."[33] There is no objective meaning in history. History is significant only to the extent that people consider it so. All history and culture is meaningful only because human beings consider it to be so.

What process occurs in order for the individual to have any objective knowledge of culture from the subjective participation in experience? It should already be clear that the idea of "objective knowledge" has a very qualified meaning in Weber's work. Objective knowledge is not to be equated with "total" or "perfect" knowledge in any way.

If the mind constructs images of reality out of the infinite complexity of experience in order to orient the individual to the empirical world, then that process is objective in the sense that subjective sensation has been processed, sorted, and categorized as *meaningful experience* by the mind. Following the Kantian epistemology, experience must be objectified before it can be turned into knowledge. Sensation must be mediated, turned into a cognition. It is different from raw sensation. Knowledge of things and events is knowledge that has gone through the process of reflection.

> Conceptual knowledge [gedankliche Erkenntnis], even of one's own experi-
> ence, is nowhere and never literally "repeated experience": of a simple "photo-
> graph" of what was experienced: the "experience" when it is made into an
> "object" acquires perspective and interrelationships which were not "known"
> in the experience itself. [34]

All experience must be mediated, processed by the mind, before it can be treated as an object of knowledge. This applies whether we are talking about our own experience or that of someone else. The process of turning subjective experience into objective reflection characterizes the acquisition of all knowledge, both in the natural and the social environment. The ideas formed in later reflection of one's own past action are no different in this respect from the ideas concerning natural events in the external world. [35]

It is clear in Weber's discussion of cognition the figure of Kant looms in the background. This model of knowledge construction makes sense only if one first accepts the Kantian notion that experience is processed by the "categories" as a means to turn simple sensation into knowledge. Kant also plays a role in Weber's discussion of the "infinite complexity" of natural and social reality. Such a position is only possible if one accepts the limits of human understanding outlined by the Kantian tradition.

However, this is not to suggest that there are not strong materialist elements in the Weberian methodology. Even with a relatively strong ontological position that stems from Kant, Weber makes it clear that it is the action of concrete individuals that make history. They seek to understand their environment and react to the forces of change within that environment. Weber is interested in what motivates those individuals to action. He leaves open what may be causally significant as he asserts it may change from epoch to epoch. He rejects any teleological conceptions of historical change and the collapsing of causality into some form of determinism.

There are no supernatural causes for historical change, except any that may exist within the subjective beliefs and psychological dispositions of the actors. Therefore, what people believe is important in explaining how people behave. These beliefs may take the form of ideological positions, religious attitudes, or subjectively held values. Any one of these, or others, may direct the action of human beings.

There is also one other component of Weber's materialism that is important to note. Consistent with the model of materialism outlined in chapter 1, the subjective character of beliefs and values severs the link between human behavior, ethics, and some conception of transcendent, universal, natural law. In contrast to the Kantian system, Weber rejects the transcendental character of ethics. It is to that topic the discussion will now turn.

Materialism and Subjective Values

Weber's analysis of the role of values is based on a clear distinction between "facts" and "values" in all forms of communication. Weber asserted that there is a logical distinction between statements that describe what "is" and those statements which judge the "appropriateness" of a given state of affairs. [36] Value judgments are to be understood as the " . . . practical evaluations of the unsatisfactory or satisfactory character of phenomena subject to our influence." [37]

Values have a pivotal role in orienting the individual to the environment. Creative intuition is the mind's mechanism to confront and make sense out of the experience of the environment. But, what is it that causes the organism to seek orientation in some areas and not in others? We seek orientation in areas of life that we consider important. Values assist in sorting through the complexity of experience itself because "[l]ife with its irrational reality and its store of possible meanings is inexhaustible." [38] Therefore, value commitments are an essential part of the personality. They assist in orienting the individual to the environment. "The light which emanates from those highest evaluative ideas always falls on an ever changing finite segment of the vast chaotic stream of events, which flows away through time." [39] Values provide a form of continuity in a world of inexhaustible sensation.

Just as the individual finds personal meaning through the adherence to values, so the social sciences are made "significant" in relation to the values that give a study its meaning. Weber was never to claim that values could be removed from social research. Quite the contrary is actually the case.

> In the empirical social sciences, . . . the possibility of meaningful knowledge . . . is bound up with the unremitting application of viewpoints . . . [which] are oriented on the basis of evaluative ideas . . . but their validity cannot be deduced from empirical data as such. [40]

Values cannot be eliminated from social research because the motivation of the investigator has its origins in his or her value positions. Our desire to confront certain aspects of our experience through social science is explained by what we consider valuable. It needs to be added here that Weber is not

suggesting that social science is strictly an arena for competing value positions. Social science is not the assertion of mere opinion. The task of social
science is the assertion of hypotheses that can be empirically demonstrated,
but have their significance bound to the value positions of the investigator.

"Importance," "significance," and "meaning" result from value commitments. Weber wants to make social science as value-free as possible, but he
recognizes that the influence of values in social research cannot be completely eliminated. Therefore, much of the discussion of values is to show the
ways in which values enter the process of social scientific investigation.
Given Weber's acceptance of an infinitely complex external reality, the influence of values in social research is a necessary condition for confining the
domain of discourse.

The individual is the repository of values. Although values may be shared
by individuals in a collective setting, only the material human being can
possess and orient behavior according to them. For this reason, Weber
claimed that social action must always be explained as the action of individuals.

> [T]he subjective interpretation of action . . . must be treated as "solely" the
> resultant . . . of particular acts of individual persons, since these alone can be
> treated as agents in a course of subjectively understandable action. . . . [T]here
> is no such thing as a collective personality which "acts."[41]

This claim was not a matter of convenience for social explanation. It is,
rather, an ontological assertion about the character of the individual and the
nature of meaningful action. Only organic life has the prerequisites for experience and the ability to reflect upon it. Only human beings can acquire and
act according to values.

If values are the results of a need for ethical orientation, out of what
process does the content of value commitments emerge? Weber gave a very
clear answer: "the highest ideals, which move us most forcefully, are always
formed only in the struggle with other ideals which are just as sacred to
others as ours are to us."[42] The reason for the struggle of value position is
also clearly enunciated by Weber. There is no objective way to verify and
validate value positions. It can certainly not be achieved through the social
sciences. The validity of any value position cannot be demonstrated by science. "It can never be the task of an empirical science to provide binding
norms and ideals . . . "[43] " . . . [T]o judge the validity of such values is a
matter of faith."[44] Weber suggested that we all have some "meta-empirical"
faith in the validity of our ultimate and final values.[45]

With no objective criteria for assessing the appropriateness of any value
position the individual is left to formulate his or her own attitude toward the
world. Meaning and significance cannot be found transcendentally, nor can

an "appropriate" attitude be found in relation to history. Values are subjectively held and formed in relation to the attitudes one encounters in society and culture.

Therefore, every individual's value position may be different. The result is tension and conflict. "Every meaningful value judgement about someone else's aspirations must be . . . a struggle against another's ideals from the standpoint of one's own."[46] Life is an unceasing struggle of value positions.

> Conflict cannot be excluded from social life. One can change its means, its objects, even its fundamental direction and its bearers, but it cannot be eliminated . . . It is always present.[47]

Or, as Weber put it in the essay, "The Logic of the Cultural Sciences:"

> [S]o long as life remains immanent and is interpreted in its own terms, it knows only of an unceasing struggle of these gods with one another. Or speaking directly, the ultimate possible attitudes toward life are irreconcilable, and hence their struggle can never be brought to a final conclusion.[48]

Life is immanent and interpreted in its own terms. There is no external objective position from which norms and values can be constructed. There is only the materiality of existence, the psychological dispositions of the participants, and the desire to understand where we have come from and where we are going.

The subjective nature of values and their importance to human life led Weber to another conclusion. "[I]t is necessary to make a decisive choice" among these competing value positions.[49] Choosing among competing value alternatives defines the personality. The validity of values themselves comes from the fact that the personality can chose to organize its life around them.[50] For Weber, this is part of the character of life itself, and a component of life that bestows meaning and significance on the individual.[51]

The Materiality of Historical Change

It is often argued that Weber has a "great man" theory of historical change. This is largely true. However, there is no necessary tension between this view and a material understanding of reality. If we accept that human beings are material creatures, then the assertion that they are the source of historical transformation does not commit an offense against a materialist world-view. Even with Weber's hard ontology, the materiality of change remains. In fact, if one accepts Weber's general epistemological stance, there is a very strong commitment to the material explanations of historical change.

In *The Social Psychology of World Religions*, Weber makes the following statement, "Not ideas, but material and ideal interests directly govern men's conduct."[52] Here Weber is trying to expand the idea of what constitutes the domain of human motivations beyond pure economic calculation. To Weber, the commitments of individuals to spiritual and religious ideals during the Middle Ages has to be taken into account in order to understand what is causally sufficient during that period. In the modern age, one would need to address the commitment to the nation-state, modern culture, and the scientific world-view in order to make sense of historical change. These patterns of belief constitute the cultural background for the formation of evaluative ideas at any point in history.

In trying to broaden the array of value commitments that motivate people to action, Weber is trying to both broaden the potentials for empirical study and convey something about the human personality. What motivates human beings to action may change in the course of history. In contrast to Marx, economic explanations may not, in all cases, be the decisive elements in explaining social change.[53]

If human beings are seen as being motivated by values, in addition to material interest, there is a much broader array of potential drives for human behavior. Further, if values are not objectively determined by history but are the result of cultural norms and social conditions in which they are formed, then there are material premises to the formation of these values in the real conditions of social existence. Values need not be treated as fully autonomous choices of *free will*, but neither do they need to be treated as fully determined by an objective process in history. For example, religiosity or patriotism may be motivators to action just as much of the economic factors in history.

The materiality of this claim is in the fact that the individual is the repository of these commitments. Only individuals think, feel, and act, even though they can create "collective action" through the coordination of their shared interests. To Weber, then, it seems natural that the carrier of historical change remains the individual.

History has no intrinsic values. It contains no teleology, no goal or objective. It can pronounce no values, and can assert no inevitable path. "History" is only the term that human beings assign to their interpretive understanding of the events that have brought them to their present condition. Only human beings have the ability to have a feeling or assessment of that condition.

The need for historical transformation occurs when human beings have come to an assessment that the current set of conditions is insufficient to satisfy their ideal or material interests. At this point the conditions for social transformation present themselves. However, this can be carried out only by the actions of discrete individuals. Here the notion of charisma is important to Weber's understanding of change.

"In this purely empirical and value-free sense charisma is indeed the specifically creative revolutionary force of history."[54] Charisma is a "special gift of body and mind" that is perceived in an individual by their followers.[55] Charismatic leaders emerge in times of social distress. Followers are compelled to search for a solution to the distress in their historical epoch. Charismatic figures provide a new orientation, or prophesy, around which the followers can organize their actions. This new prophesy's value is that it provides a conceptual reorientation for the people to their social, political, or environmental conditions.

Revolutionary change has its source in the perceptions of concrete human beings in the world. These perceptions are going to be shaped by a multitude of factors owing to the differing values and material interests of society's members. But for Weber, when it comes to social action, only individuals can move individuals in a new direction. The new rational orientation is a product of human creativity coupled with the desire for a new direction among a collection of individual followers.

The Materiality of Power

There are two elements of Weber's work on political power that are worth noting in relation to materialism. The first is the way in which Weber seeks to study power and the workings of what can generally be called "politics." The second concerns the content of Weber's statements about politics. Weber can be characterized as a "realist" when it comes to the definition of power and its role inside society. Further, as power is directly connected to what motivates people to action, its materiality cannot be denied.

Much has already been stated about Weber's method, but a few additional observations regarding its material premises are worth noting. In the study of political power Weber looks for material reference points. In seeking to explain migration patterns in West Prussia Weber engages data on tax yields from the land, data on social stratification, population density, religious and national affiliations, as well as a host of other demographic and economic data.[56] The point here is simply that even if one does not accept the hard ontology that is part of Weber's personal orientation, the methodology is empirically focused to such a degree that the ontological position does not have a major impact on the method of social research. For example, one of Weber's conclusions in the study of West Prussia is that the pursuit of freedom is a motivator to migration, but even this is not treated as an abstraction. Freedom is treated as the ability to create a set of conditions to improve the living standards for people engaged in migratory activity.[57]

Regarding the definition of political power, Weber gives a statement that speaks to the material elements of power. Power is the ability for someone to carry out their will despite resistance.[58] When it comes to the state's relationship with power, Weber asserted that the state is founded on power, and has a monopoly on the legitimate use of force within its territory.[59]

But politics is not asserted to have any historical dynamics driving it in a particular direction. Instead, power is seen as a manifestation of political life. The direction of collective action results from the struggles among competing material and ideal interests. The tensions and struggles are everywhere in the political and social environment. The logic of capitalism is in a state of tension with the sublime values of brotherliness contained in religion.[60] The rise of bureaucracy conflicts with the worth of the individual in society.[61] Money and wealth are part of a political dynamic that can undermine democratic practice and can shape the outcome of political competitions.[62] Even the scientific method creates the conditions of normlessness and social anomie. In discussing the loss of purpose in modern scientific culture, Weber states that "culture's every step forward seems condemned to lead to an ever more devastating senselessness."[63] All of these examples convey the complex cross-currents in modern culture.

The closest Weber comes to some conclusions about the future of political life come in his observations about the future of individualism in a formally rational, bureaucratized society. These same discussions take place at both the end of the *Protestant Ethic* and *Economy and Society*. However, to Weber these are empirically based observations that relate to research that Max carried out with his brother, Alfred, going back to the late nineteenth century.

For Weber, these and the myriad of other observations about the workings of society, politics, and history have their basis in observable, empirical phenomena. Does that mean that every hypothesis that emerges from this process of analysis will be complete and correct? Such a position is rejected by Weber. His claim is simply that as an investigator he must look to the empirical evidence and make a plausible case for what he sees as a trend based on the selective interpretation of the historical facts. This is the basic way all social inquiry is conducted. There will be other, competing, interpretations. Such is the nature of all investigations into the actions found in our social environment.

Weber's Materialism: An Assessment

To assess Weber's contribution to materialism a distinction must be made between his view of science and his view of social science. Science, to Weber, is the study of regularities among the non-animate objects of physical reality. Science seeks to create hypotheses that explain the regularity of the patterns found among those physical objects. The subject of social science is fundamentally different. Its domain is the study of beings that are simultaneously both subject and object. Not only does Weber's methodology account for this distinction, it seeks to do so in a very self-conscious way.

Weber's methodological system is complex and powerful. It occupies a kind of middle ground between phenomenology and empiricism. It manages to account for the development of consciousness as a psychological disposition toward the external environment, and still stress the fundamental role of empirical phenomena in constructing causal and non-causal relationships in social reality.

Key to understanding the empirical reference points is the Kantian idea that our experiences are always mediated, in the sense that our mind turns direct experience into cognitions. In this sense, experience may be a direct cause of human action, like moving out of the way of a rolling boulder, or a person putting up an umbrella in a rain storm. However, as Weber makes clear, these are not social actions. Social actions are oriented toward the behavior of other human beings.

Thus, when one considers social action it must always be in relation to the material and ideal interests maintained by human beings. As with Marx, this means that ideas can be the motivators to actions as they represent a subjectively held understanding about social reality and the way it functions. However, Weber broadens the field of what may be causally significant in explaining historical change.

Further, rather than fixing the factors that are relevant to historical change, as is the case with Marx, Weber relativizes the important factors initiating historical transformation. In each age and in each culture the factors that are causally significant may change. This makes the study of social reality far more complex, requiring investigators to explore the infinite richness of causal connections for each historical or cultural event they seek to study. Such a position clearly moves Weber in the direction of epistemological relativism and furthers his materialist credentials. Furthering those credentials is Weber's insistence that the explanations of social reality are always hypothetical and subject to multiple interpretations. Scientific syntax produces only hypotheses, whether in the physical or the social realm. Therefore, there can be no universal truth. This is the same for physical and social science, although, Weber does not address the full relativity of science.

The discussion of ethics and values is where relativism fully emerges. The individual personality makes its mark in the world by taking a value position toward that world. These values are shaped by the social experiences that one has in the formation of those values. Science cannot tell us what values to hold. They are subjective commitments that reflect the historical, social, and cultural influences in which an individual finds themselves in the process of their growth and development.

This position constitutes one of Weber's major breaks with Kant. The Kantian ethics relies on an assumption of free will as a universal human faculty and the formation of natural law principles formulated on that assumption. Weber clearly rejects that position. In a section of *Economy and*

Society focused on the topic of natural law, Weber gives a definition, a survey of the history of its use, and a description of its sociological relevance. Discussions of natural law are relevant from a sociological standpoint only to the extent to which they give rise to "practical consequences." That is, "[T]hey become sociologically relevant only when practical legal life is materially affected by the conviction of the particular 'legitimacy' of certain legal maxims . . . "[64] After noting that this idea still has impact in the United State,[65] Weber goes on to say:

> While it would hardly seem possible to eradicate completely from legal practice all the latent influence of unacknowledged axioms of natural law, for a variety of reasons the axioms of natural law have been deeply discredited. . . . All metajuristic axioms in general have been subject to ever continuing disintegration and relativization. . . . The disappearance of the old natural law conceptions has destroyed all possibility of providing the law with a metaphysical dignity by virtue of its immanent qualities.[66]

Such a claim is not just about natural law. All metaphysical explanations of the world are being discredited by the march of rational, material culture. This is part of the general process of "disenchantment" that Weber discusses in "Science as a Vocation." Metaphysical explanations of the world are being replaced with a materialist understanding of the world. Such a condition reflects the current world culture.

This leaves people with both a problem and a choice. Ancient metaphysics lacks the validity of empirical discourse. However, modern science cannot answer the question of how we should live. Therefore, each has to make a choice as to what is god and what is devil in our daily lives.[67]

Clearly such a broad array of societal factors in the formation of value commitments would include the reward structures in the political system as well as the creation of complex systems of programming and propaganda that exist within the nation-state system, as well as the conditions of capitalist development. Weber does not give an extensive elaboration of all those mechanisms. Nevertheless, he clearly shows sensitivity to the materiality of the process.

In this regard, Weber also demonstrates a clear position on the materiality of power. Weber is not an anarchist. He believes that power can be converted into authority through a logic of legitimation. The legitimacy of that power resides in the belief among the followers that their interests are served by following its directives. This is the case for all the legitimating mechanisms of power that Weber mentions: charismatic, traditional, or rational-legal.

From the perspective of politics, this means that there is also relativity introduced into the realm of power and politics. There is no simple linear notion of political progress in Weber. In contrast to Kant, constitutions do not simply beget better constitutions through the span of time. Change can be initiated from an infinite array of causal factors. The beliefs of the population may be transformed and a different mix of legitimating mechanisms may emerge. There is no final teleology reached with constitutional democracy. Weber admits to a variety of possibilities for the future.

But the question how of far Weber separates himself from Kant remains an issue. Weber is clearly influenced by the Kantian epistemology. What about Kant's ontology? Weber treats the content of consciousness as being altered by historical conditions but not the fundamental makeup of human nature. He still has a static view of human nature, even while acknowledging the flux of historical dynamics. The social world is dominated by the search for individual freedom. Self-transcendence comes through creative intuition and personal commitments. One would have to consider this "hard ontology" that contains elements that are ahistorical in nature.

Are these assumptions metaphysical in nature? It is undeniable that there are metaphysical elements here. Here Max Weber and Jacques Derrida agree, albeit for slightly different reasons. For Derrida, it is impossible to get all the metaphysics out of our discourse. For Weber, assumptions cannot be escaped. Even science itself rests on presuppositions and norms, the worth of which cannot be demonstrated by science. [68]

CONCLUSION

Weber is interested in creating a method of social research that is as materialistic and as objective as possible. To that end, he employs empirical methods but is, himself, not an empiricist. To Weber, pure empiricism is too unselfconscious of its own limitations. Empiricism seeks to solidify its objectivity, hence its materiality, with reference only to that which is objectively verifiable through the senses. Empiricism focuses on behavior as the material element of analysis. It seeks to identify trends and create causal hypotheses that provide the ability to predict and control future events based on that data.

In this sense, the use of empirical methods is not inconsistent with Weber's general methodological strategy. But there are two major differences. Within the Weberian model, empiricism seems unconcerned about the limitations of objectivity. Weber went to great lengths to explain these limitations. Empiricism's focus on observed behavior does not mitigate the subjective nature of the investigator's interest and values in establishing the study. Further, it does not make self-conscious the subjective nature of indicators for any explanation of causality. Empiricism, in its pure form, simply ignores the way in which objectivity is tainted by historical and contextual biases. For Weber, social research cannot be collapsed into pure positivism or empiricism because of the influence of personal values or historically driven interests in the conduct of social research.

The other major difference concerns the goal of engaging in social research itself. Through the study of behavior, empiricism seeks to have a causal explanation of events. This can assist in the future prediction of events and, possibly, the control of outcomes. While Weber is also concerned with causality, his objective is different. Weber is interested in "understanding." This means that while he is interested in the causal sequences that explain the events of social and historical reality, he is also interested in what makes the event "subjectively meaningful." Weber wants to know not only what happened and why it happened, but his methodology is also interested in explaining why people care about the events in question. What is it that makes the event meaningful for both the participant and the observer?

Therefore, Weber's method makes both the participant and the observers subjects of inquiry, with both having subjectively meaningful engagement in the conduct of inquiry. There is an implicit relativity to such a claim. Both the subject and the investigator are placed within the context of history. Both are engaged in actions that have subjective meaning.

Weber's method was an attempt to make the social science materialistic in the sense that human beings and their behavior were the central focus of research. Human beings exist. They hold beliefs that shape their behavior. Weber always focused on the material origins of those beliefs, recognizing that human beings will always act in relation to their understanding of reality. This is true for the actors and those who study the actors in history. Determining what constitutes the "real" is, itself, always the issue.

Weber conveyed the magnitude of what is implied by a materialist understanding of the world in one of his last addresses of his life, "Science as a Vocation," presented in Munich in 1918. After stating that the gap between science and religion is "unbridgeable"[69] he goes on to speak about the materialist character of the contemporary age and the rupture it causes in modern society.

> The fate of our times is characterized by rationalization and intellectualization and, above all, by the 'disenchantment of the world.' Precisely the ultimate and most sublime values have retreated from public life either into the transcendental realm of mystic life or into the brotherliness of direct and personal human relations . . . To the person who cannot bear the fate of the times like a man, one must say: may he rather return silently, without the usual publicity build-up of renegades, but simply and plainly. The arms of the old churches are opened widely and compassionately for him.[70]

The "disenchantment of the world" is another way of saying that religious and metaphysical systems of knowledge are being replaced with a materialist understanding of both physical reality and the social institutions in which people live.

Nevertheless, one cannot read the last few pages of "Science as a Vocation" and not come away with the feeling that Weber is personally conflicted about the results of the very society that he is helping to create. The old religion welded people into communities. Modern scientific culture cannot perform that function because each must choose his or her own god.

Something is gained, and something is lost in the modern world. However, the condition of the present is clear. A materialist understanding of the world is the condition of our current culture. Weber was interested in finding the proper methods to study it.

NOTES

1. See *Romance and Reason: Ontological and Social Sources of Alienation in the Writings of Max Weber*. (Lanham, MD: Lexington Books, 2006.)

2. See "Science as a Vocation," in *From Max Weber* (New York: Oxford University Press, 1958).

3. Max Weber, *Roscher and Knies: The Logical Problems of Historical Economics* (New York: Free Press, 1975), 66-67.

4. Weber, *Roscher and Knies*, 67.

5. Weber, *Roscher and Knies*, 73-74.

6. Max Weber, *The Methodology of the Social Sciences* (New York: Free Press, 1949), 106.

7. Weber, *Roscher and Knies*, 69-72.

8. Weber, *Roscher and Knies*, 70.

9. Weber, *The Methodology of the Social Sciences*, 73-75.

10. Weber, *The Methodology of the Social Sciences*, 76.

11. Weber, *The Methodology of the Social Sciences*, 103.

12. Weber, *The Methodology of the Social Sciences*, 90.

13. Weber, *The Methodology of the Social Sciences*, 90.

14. Karl Marx, "The German Ideology," in *The Marx-Engels Reader*, edited by Robert Tucker (New York: Norton, 1978), 154.

15. Weber, *The Methodology of the Social Sciences*, 71.

16. Weber, *The Methodology of the Social Sciences*, 84.

17. Weber *The Methodology of the Social Sciences*, 106.

18. Immanuel Kant, *The Critique of Pure Reason* (New York, Modern Library, 1958), 26

19. Kant, *The Critique of Pure Reason*, 54.

20. Weber, *The Methodology of the Social Sciences*, 78.

21. Weber, "Science as a Vocation," in *From Max Weber*, 154.

22. Weber, *The Methodology of the Social Sciences*, 123.

23. Weber, *The Methodology of the Social Sciences*, 84.

24. Weber, *The Methodology of the Social Sciences*, 91.

25. Weber, *The Methodology of the Social Sciences*, 91.

26. Weber, *The Methodology of the Social Sciences*, 90.

27. Weber, *The Methodology of the Social Sciences*, 175.

28. Weber, *The Methodology of the Social Sciences*, 173-174.

29. Weber, *The Methodology of the Social Sciences*, 175.

30. Weber, Max. *Economy and Society*. (Berkeley: University of California Press, 1978), 4.

31. Weber, *Economy and Society*, 14.

32. Weber, *The Methodology of the Social Sciences*, 80.

33. Weber, *The Methodology of the Social Sciences*, 81.

34. Weber, *The Methodology of the Social Sciences*, 178.

35. Weber, *The Methodology of the Social Sciences*, 178.

36. Weber, *The Methodology of the Social Sciences*, 19.
37. Weber, *The Methodology of the Social Sciences*, 1.
38. Weber, *The Methodology of the Social Sciences*, 111.
39. Weber, *The Methodology of the Social Sciences*, 111.
40. Weber, *The Methodology of the Social Sciences*, 111.
41. Weber, *Economy and Society*, 13-14.
42. Weber, *The Methodology of the Social Sciences*, 57.
43. Weber, *The Methodology of the Social Sciences*, 52.
44. Weber, *The Methodology of the Social Sciences*, 55.
45. Weber, *The Methodology of the Social Sciences*, 111.
46. Weber, *The Methodology of the Social Sciences*, 60.
47. Weber, *The Methodology of the Social Sciences*, 26-27.
48. Weber, "Science as a Vocation" in *From Max Weber*, 152.
49. Weber, "Science as a Vocation" in *From Max Weber*, 152.
50. Weber, *The Methodology of the Social Sciences*, 55.
51. Weber *The Methodology of the Social Sciences*, 55.
52. Weber, "Social Psychology of World Religions," in *From Max Weber*, 280.
53. Weber, *The Methodology of the Social Sciences*, 1949, 68.
54. Weber, *Economy and Society*, 1117.
55. Weber, *Economy and Society*, 1112.
56. Max Weber, "The Nation State and Economic Policy," in *Weber: Political Writing* (Cambridge, UK: Cambridge University Press, 1994), 3-8.
57. Weber, "The Nation State and Economic Policy," 8.
58. Weber, *Economy and Society*, 53.
59. Weber, "Politics as a Vocation," in *From Max Weber*, 78.
60. Weber, *Economy and Society*, 138.
61. Weber, *Economy and Society*, 1402.
62. Weber, "Politics as a Vocation," in *From Max Weber*, 97.
63. Max Weber, "Religious Rejections of the World and Their Directions," in *From Max Weber*, 357.
64. Weber, *Economy and Society*, 866.
65. Weber, *Economy and Society*, 866.
66. Weber, *Economy and Society*, 874-875.
67. Weber, "Science as a Vocation" in *From Max Weber*, 148.
68. Weber, "Science as a Vocation" in *From Max Weber*, 143.
69. Weber, "Science as a Vocation" in *From Max Weber*, 154.
70. Weber, "Science as a Vocation" in *From Max Weber*, 155.

Chapter Five

Nietzsche

Materialism and the Human Animal

INTRODUCTION

For the last 2,500 years, Western civilization has been engaged in an intellectual exercise to lift human beings out of the animal kingdom. Central to this undertaking is the view that human beings, because they have a "consciousness," are qualitatively different than the other species that inhabit the planet. Their bodies are repositories of this consciousness, the way a bottle is the vessel for the liquid it carries. Consciousness and matter are different, with consciousness as the repository of reason, morality, and knowledge.

Plato not only exemplifies this attitude in the doctrine of the forms but emphasizes the significance of reason as the tool for the undoing of our animal nature. Reason is the source of control over our irrational instincts. The extent of reason's control over the impulsive side of the human character represents the measure of our growth as a species. Only when this is achieved is one truly the master of the self and able to transcend the materiality of existence. Then one can understand the true foundation for stable and unchanging truths in the world.

The rise of Christianity offered another method for the employment of fixed and static truths. God descends into the world either directly or through prophets and reveals the ideals and practices that are part of His will in the world. God's intention is to save mankind through the delivery of an unchanging set of rules and practices that are the path to human salvation.

In the modern period, Immanuel Kant moderates this position. He suggests that human beings do not have direct access to the transcendent realm but can reason its existence. Further, because of the contrast between thought and sensation, and the fact that human beings possess both faculties, it is suggested that there is something transcendent within the mind/body dualism that is our ontological makeup. This transcendent arena, the noumenal, presents a domain of possibilities, as it is the domain of both reason and freedom. "Free will" can thus be saved from the clutches of pure empiricism. Reason can ascend to discover what is true and universal within the transcendent realm. Our social and political aspirations can then then be constructed in a way to conform to the truth acquired through reason.

However, suppose we move in another direction. Suppose we think deeply about what the model of human evolution outlined by Darwin really means. What do all the constructions of moral codes, teleologies of history, and natural law look like from the perspective of a species that evolved like all others? What if it is not possible to leave our animal natures behind? What if we are just another form of animal that evolves like all others? If that is the case, our philosophic and social history has been little more than a trail of lies.

This is precisely the position of Friedrich Nietzsche. In Nietzsche's view, he is peeling off the mask that has been used to cover the character of human existence. Central to Nietzsche's exploration is evolutionary biology. Nietzsche repeatedly invokes Darwin, and even when Nietzsche offers criticism of Darwin, it is still Darwin's biology that influences Nietzsche's thought. To Nietzsche we are now in a new age. All that has been carried from the past much be rethought and regrounded, if it can be, within a new intellectual paradigm.

THE MATERIALITY OF THE KNOWLEDGE

Although Nietzsche criticizes Darwin in numerous places, he accepts Darwin's basic premise that human beings evolved on the earth. Evolution is embedded in our organic existence.

> The astral arrangement in which we live is an exception; this arrangement, and the relatively long durability which is determined by it, has again made possible the exception of exceptions, the formation of organic life.[1]

To adjust itself to its environment, organic life adapts and changes. The human organism has developed a capacity for knowledge. However, to Nietzsche that capacity is sorely limited.

> Once upon a time, in some out of the wary corner of that universe which is dispersed into numberless twinkling solar systems, there was a star upon which clever beasts invented knowing . . . One might invent such a fable, and yet he still would not have adequately illustrated how miserable, how shadowy

and transient, how aimless and arbitrary the human intellect looks within nature.[2]

To Nietzsche there is no separation of mind and body. The brain evolved as a part of the body that assisted in the preservation of the species.

> In order for a particular species to maintain itself and increase its power, its conception of reality must comprehend enough of the calculable and constant for it to base a scheme of behavior on it. The utility of preservation—not some abstract-theoretical need not to be deceived—stands as the motive behind the development of the organs of knowledge—they develop in such a way that their observations suffice for our preservation.[3]

As a result, Nietzsche concludes that the understanding of the world created by our body's thinking organ cannot capture what is universal or transcendental because we are historically bound creatures. When Nietzsche speaks of "truth," he is referring to that which is fixed and eternal. But to Nietzsche, truth is an illusion we have created for ourselves. There is no "truth" in the human experience.

The senses provide us with impressions of the external environment. However, the senses only provide the raw material for concepts. They do not teach us the truth of a thing.[4] They provide the basis for our interpretations of the world. Everything we become aware of is only an interpretation.[5]

Our thoughts do not capture essences, entertain revelations supplied by a deity, or ascend to universal moral knowledge. We create knowledge that serves our needs. This means that our intellectual capacity is limited to "interpretation."[6]

> There exists neither "spirit," nor reason, nor thinking, nor consciousness, nor soul, nor will, nor truth: all are fictions that are of no use. There is no question of "subject and object," but of a particular species of animal that can prosper only through a certain relative rightness; above all, regularity of its perceptions (so that it can accumulate experience) . . .[7]

Therefore, truth eludes us. Our minds are not capable of such power. Truth cannot be found or discovered. Our knowledge is always human-centric, a reflection of our needs coupled with our limited capacities.[8]

Nietzsche's point is that as biological creatures we have a need to adjust our material activities to the realities of the world. In the process, we create an understanding of that world which we code into narratives. These narratives are not reality, but are illusions that we identify as truths, or universals, when we are, in fact, incapable of such constructions.

> What then is truth? A movable host of metaphors, metonymies, and anthropomorphisms: In short, a sum of human relations which have been poetically and

rhetorically intensified, transferred, and embellished, and which, after long
usage, seem to a people to be fixed, canonical, and binding. Truths are illusions which we have forgotten are illusions . . . [9]

These illusions have their origins in necessity. We have to adjust ourselves to
the external world as part of the mechanism of survival. [10] But our illusions
are aesthetic judgments, not an uncovering of the secrets found in the universe. This is the case even for physics, which Nietzsche identifies as an
interpretive enterprise as well. [11] Put another way, we are creatures that must
interpret our reality to survive. We do not uncover truth.

We need knowledge, but we need to keep in mind that it is always "human knowledge," not knowledge per se. Knowledge construction, therefore,
is always an anthropomorphic enterprise. "At bottom, what the investigator
of such truths is seeking is only the metamorphosis of the world into man." [12]
This is carried out through the construction of concepts and their repetition in
language. [13]

> Even the relationship of a nerve stimulus to the generated image is not a
> necessary one. But when the same image has been generated millions of time
> and has been handed down for many generations and finally appears on the
> same occasion every time for all mankind, then it acquires at last the same
> meaning for men it would if it were the sole necessary image and if the
> relationship of the original nerve stimulus to the generated image were a
> strictly causal one. In the same manner, an eternally repeated dream would
> certainly be felt and judged to be reality. [14]

Our understanding of the world is a product of what is repeated as truth
within the culture. It is a matter of what "circulates." There is no correspondence between what is presented as "object" and our interpretation of it.
There are no a priori truths. [15] There are no facts. There are only interpretations. [16]

The critique of Western epistemology constitutes a major part of Nietzsche's materialist perspective. Since the beginning of civilization human beings have been constructing an evolving narrative of who they are, their
essential characteristics, and an illusory understanding of the universal character of the moral codes that have directed their behavior. None of this is
possible in the wake of Nietzsche's critique.

GENEALOGY AS MATERIALIST METHODOLOGY

The method Nietzsche employs is genealogy. Gilles Deleuze calls genealogy
Nietzsche's method to study the origin of values. [17] However, the genealog-
ical method can be used to uncover much more than the origin of values. It is
Nietzsche's method to uncover the origins of what human beings believe

about themselves, the world, and their social and political practices. In general, it is a materialist methodology employed to uncover the material origins of what people think and how they behave. The major work that displays this methodological approach is *The Genealogy of Morals*.

In *The Genealogy of Morals* Nietzsche is asking a simple question: How did human beings come to believe in certain moral prescriptions? Such a question always has a corollary. It must also address what human beings have to believe about themselves in order to make those moral prescriptions *rational*? What Nietzsche is trying to convey is that the pronouncement of what people believe is not enough for a full understanding of the power and dimensions of those beliefs. There needs to be an entire substratum of assumptions, constructions, and illusions in order to make the belief *rational* in the eyes of the actors.

The genealogical method attempts to do this by performing two tasks: giving an empirically based hypothesis about the material origin of a belief or practice, and drawing the connections between that belief or practice to a larger set of ideas about human subjectivity and the nature of social reality. All this must be accomplished without reference to a transcendent subject, fixed canonical norms, and stable universal values. This is a tall order, and while Nietzsche may stray over the materialist line at times with regard to his own conclusions about subjectivity, the methodological strategy remains clear.

If an utterance does not capture truth, it is a reflection of cultural conditioning, subjective interests, or both. Therefore, the exploration of moral positions cannot be separated from the rules of language. Further, since the medium of language is always mediated within the context of social forces present in the society, these utterances must also be considered political acts.

Nietzsche focuses on the control of language as a manifestation of political power. In ancient times, this meant that values were a reflection of the nobility.[18] However, a transvaluation of values occurred as Christianity spread among the multitudes of the poor and the powerless. They were "seduced" by a belief system that placed them at the center of the moral universe. Their numbers gave them political power and their ideas political direction. They invented democracy and democratic values as a manifestation of that power.

Therefore, it was not the *truth* of Christianity that was its appeal, but timeliness of its message to a Roman society in which poverty and depravity had run its course. The transformation from Roman polytheism to Christianity was a political manifestation of class distinctions. Christianity appealed to a growing number of poor. It both explained their plight and promised them salvation. As the number of believers increased so did their power to transform the culture. Aristocratic ideals were replaced with what Nietzsche refers to as a slave mentality. The inferior dragged society down to its level. Guilt, blame, fear, and the will to smallness are the hallmarks of this culture.

One can quibble with some of the sweeping generalities, provocative pronouncements, and the conspiratorial nature of some of the claims of the *Genealogy*. However, to focus on such things would be to miss the point. Nietzsche is seeking to provide a methodology for the generation of knowledge about the origins of beliefs and practices that does not require the construction of a subject prior to the analysis. He claims that moral conscience has its origin, not in truth, but in objective experience of history along with the likes and dislikes of those with power.[19] This means that Western philosophy has been a fruitless enterprise.

> In all "science of morals" so far one thing was lacking, strange as it may sound: the problem of morality itself; what was lacking was any suspicion that there was something problematic here. What the philosophers called "a rational foundation for morality" and tried to supply was, seen in the right light, merely a scholarly variation of the common faith in the prevalent morality; a new means of expression of this faith; and thus just another fact within a particular morality; indeed, in the last analysis a kind of denial that this morality might ever be considered problematic . . .[20]

It is hard not to imagine Nietzsche having Kant in mind when he wrote this. To Nietzsche, subjectivity reflects its context. Organic life adjusts itself to its conditions. Human beings adjust their beliefs to the conditions presented by necessity.

Genealogy begins with the practice or belief and asks, "What does one have to believe about oneself in order to make this rational?" Therefore, even as the constructions of the self are illusory, they can still be analyzed for their content and for their material origins. In this way, we can study the human experience through studying the residue of culture. Morality is a symptom to be read.[21] The real question is what do moralities tell us about their creators.[22] The truth of what a human being is remains illusory. Nevertheless, Nietzsche's method seeks to show the process of how we invent those illusions. It also seeks to maintain a materialist character in the process.

This perspective is at the core of the genealogical method. Genealogy begins with the assumption that human beings do not create truths, but utilities. Morality must be read as one of those utilities. Therefore, the question can never be, "what is the content of human morality?" The question is instead, "what is the utility of this or that moral code?" Who is speaking? Whose interest is being served? Morality never tells us about universal truth. It tells us about the character and needs of its creators.[23]

Nietzsche has stripped the human being naked and asked: What remains? The challenge is to provide an explanation that fits into the parameters of his epistemological understanding of what is possible. That means that the explanation must be consistent with: the anthropomorphic character of knowledge, the inability to fix and define human nature and subjectivity (while allowing for open evolutionary development), a recognition of *necessity* as the origin of ethics and morality, and a generally relativizing understanding of reality. This is a tall order.

Genealogy is a materialist methodology to study all the beliefs and practices in which human beings are engaged. This covers not just the formation of human's moral beliefs, but would also include the beliefs that animate their social and political institutions. Sovereignty, patriotism, capitalism, rational administration, and a host of other beliefs and practices can be analyzed using this method. It is a method that asks, "what are the conditions that gave rise to such beliefs?" It will be of particular interest to Michel Foucault.

THE MATERIALITY OF INSTINCTS

To this point, the focus of this chapter has largely been directed toward the limitations Nietzsche places on our ability to know. But Nietzsche is also trying to direct his readers to an understanding of the instincts that he says are present in the human being, lying under the surface. Animal life is directed by drives and instincts.

Is it possible for Nietzsche to retain his materialist credentials and to provide more in terms of an understanding of his views on human activity? What motivates human beings to action? Is it only survival? What is left after the genealogical method has stripped away our illusions?

The *subject* is an invention.[24] As such, the notion of subjectivity cannot serve as the foundation for an understanding of human beings. Therefore, Nietzsche looks to human behavior and the motivations to behavior as the telltale signs as to the nature of human beings. Behavior is the measure of the human story. " . . . [T]here is no 'being' behind doing, effecting, becoming; 'the doer' is merely a fiction added to the deed—the deed is everything."[25]

Subjectivity is a construction that has a double purpose. It is an addendum to the array of human actions that allows for the action to appear *rational* within the frame of human activity and for the action to be judged as appropriate or moral against the constructed standard. This duel function gives the construction of subjectivity a powerful role in the social structures. Punishment then takes on a dual character as well. It has the function of enforcing compliance with expected norms and functions to reinforce the dominant narrative on subjectivity through the imposition of its content.

Such a disciplinary scheme would not be possible without the invention of *free will*, in either Christian or Kantian varieties. To Nietzsche, free will was invented by the rulers and priests in order to allow punishment.[26] It has no standing as *truth*, something even Kant admitted, but its transmission over the centuries has been an essential tool to the ruling elites. Each can be made accountable, because each is an independent moral agent. In this way, the construction of subjectivity can be maintained.

So the notion of *will* as a transcendentally free, creative, or moral force in human beings is rejected by Nietzsche. Such traits are never assigned to other creatures in the animal kingdom. We do not consider snails or jellyfish to possess will. Why is it assigned to human beings?

> We no longer derive man from "the spirit" or "the deity"; we have placed him back among the animals. We consider him the strongest animal because he is the most cunning . . . On the other hand, we oppose the vanity that would raise its head again here too—as if man had been the great hidden purpose of the evolution of the animals. Man is by no means the crown of creation; every living being stands beside him on the same level of perfection. [27]

As animals, human beings have drives, passions, and psychological states that motivate them to action, but of which they are scarcely aware. It would be false to assume that instincts drive the rest of the animal kingdom, but such forces are not found within the human being.

The discussion of these drives and instincts by Nietzsche is complex and nuanced. It is significant for both what he says about the will, and what he rejects within the history of ideas. The summation of all these drives Nietzsche terms "the will to power."

> Suppose, finally, we succeeded in explaining our entire instinctive life as the development and ramification of one basic form of the will—namely, the will to power, as my proposition has it; suppose all organic functions could be traced back to this will to power and one could also find in it the solution of the problem of procreation and nourishment—it is one problem—then one would have gained the right to determine all efficient force univocally as—will to power. [28]

Life is the will to power. [29] It involves all organic functions. [30] But the will to power is not representative of one human instinct but a term used to summarize a multiplicity of instincts and drives. It is the drive to self-preservation, the drive to knowledge, to procreation, to creativity, and a host of other motivations to action. It is not, as Nietzsche makes clear, the will to control others. [31]

Therefore, the self is defined as a complex of competing drives. What manifests as behavior is the effective outcome of that struggle. Nietzsche claims that it is a mistake to assume that the intellect has sorted and analyzed the possible states and chosen an outcome. That would place the intellect in opposition and control of instincts. What we consider the "intellect" is actually an invention to mask the operation of instincts. The effect is always a result of the "behavior of the instincts toward one another."[32]

So what is *will* in this scheme? Nietzsche uses the term often. He clearly rejects the idea of free will.[33] Our drives and desires are not even the result of individual wills, but psychological motivations that are part of human instincts. The individuality that is often attributed to Nietzsche is manifested in the fact that individuals have differing levels of will through which they express those instincts. Superior individuals express their instincts as creativity and do so more effectively than inferiors.

Here a question that needs to be asked regarding the impact of this position on Nietzsche's materialist credentials. Does the characterization of life as the "will to power" constitute a hard ontological positon that would undermine Nietzsche's status as a materialist? Such a case could be argued.

However, Nietzsche makes no grand statements about consciousness that are tied to such claims. In fact, he considers human consciousness to be quite underdeveloped.[34] Taken as a general statement about the animated nature of life coupled with the character of our biological motives to action, the will to power is not a grand ontological statement, but a characterization of what it means to be alive. Life grows, expands, consumes, and creates as part of its materiality in the world. This is part of our material *being* in the world.

Nietzsche proposes a *naturalistic* morality that is dominated by the instincts of life.[35] Natural morality embraces the will to power in all its forms. The will to power is an event or activity in which life seeks to extend its force.[36]

> My idea is that every specific body strives to become master over all space and to extend its force (its will to power) and to thrust back all that resists its extension. But it continually encounters similar efforts on the part of other bodies and ends by coming to an arrangement ("union") with those of them that are sufficiently related to it; thus they then conspire together for power. And the process goes on . . .[37]

One can read this as an expression of life, as it seeks to expand its reach as an expression of itself as life. Or one can read this as a statement about the nature of social and political life. Social and political institutions emerge in the compromise of human life seeking to extend itself in a condition in which others are doing the same. Political balance, of sorts, becomes the outcome. Both interpretations are, in the end, reflections of the same process. Both serve the will to power.

But Nietzsche's discussion of morality is not simply a critique of the foundations of the old morality nor a genealogical discussion of its origins. Evolutionary biology suggests that a new order of moral is not only desirable, but also necessary. In *Zarathustra* a new morality is heralded with the coming of the *übermensch*. However, this will need to be put in context.

Nietzsche believes that the old religion is being overwhelmed and undermined by science. Religion cannot hold up to the epistemological critique that results from science's demands for empirical referents within scientific syntax. For this reason, Zarathustra comes down from the mountain and pronounces the death of God. The death of God is obviously not an empirical statement, but a statement regarding the material force of the concept *God* as a motivation or justification for human action. As a foundational principle supporting morals, God's death means the moral pillars that supported the Christian morality, and the pseudo-Christian morality of Kant, collapse.

It is for this reason Nietzsche spoke of a coming age of nihilism, an age where the old order had died but a new order of morality had not yet emerged.[38] "I write for a species of man that does not yet exist . . . "[39] A transvaluation of values as significant as the one brought about by the Christian order is now necessary. However, it has to be based on the characteristic of the human being as an animal in the world, a being that is shaped by the order of evolutionary biology.

The old morality attacked passion. Such morality is anti-life.[40] It sought to assign guilt and blame. Each is responsible. All owe a debt.[41] Such a view looks to the past. We must consider the future not the past.[42] We need to train people for heights, not mediocrity.[43]

That means a new foundation for moral claims must be created. "If the morality of 'thou shalt not lie' is rejected, the 'sense for truth' will have to legitimize itself before another tribunal: as a means of the preservation of man, as the will to power."[44] The "scientific outlook" can assist in our understanding of the behavior that is consistent with our survival and growth.[45] Morality can be created for its biological utility rather than its employment of ancient texts.[46]

We need a morality that is constructed after we have been placed back among the animals. It must recognize that there are no "moral facts."[47] There are only moral utilities for a species that seeks to survive and grow within its environment. "What is good? Everything that heightens the feeling of power in man, the will to power, power itself."[48]

One final point is worth noting. Nietzsche never viewed the lack of transcendent knowledge and morality a cause for despair. Rather, human beings should celebrate, finally acknowledging that they have the power to shape the future. "The problem I thus pose is not what shall succeed mankind in the sequence of living beings (man is an end), but what type of man shall be bred, shall be willed, for being higher in value, worthier of life, more certain of a future."[49] As biological creatures the world can be in our hands and the future shaped by that condition.

GENEALOGY AND THE MATERIAL ANALYSIS OF CULTURE

Our understanding of the world is an entirely human creation. Yet it is not the product of a single individual or generation. We carry the camel's burden from one generation to the next. The medium of that process is language.

The "word" is a nerve stimuli.[50] When the organism has a sensation it creates a word for that sensation. From the collection of words, concepts are built.[51] Concepts designate cases where there are similar characteristics.[52] But Nietzsche is concerned for what is missing in this formulation. When a concept is created it dulls the differences among the discrete events that make up its domain. The uniqueness of each case is lost to the general. We become conditioned to think in terms of similarities rather than differences.

We think in the form that language provides for us.[53] Every effect must have a cause. Every event must have a rational explanation. We cannot think outside the parameters set by the rules of language.[54] Our language creates the illusion that our impressions have stability and the harmony of their commonality is greater than the discord of their difference.

However, our language is metaphorical. It does not capture the truth of the Kantian thing-in-itself. It conveys a story. Our understanding of the world is an aesthetic phenomenon.[55] The construction of subjectivity is part of that story. So is the construction of culture.

Culture, as the collection of beliefs and practices, gives meaning to the vast number of people in society. It is central to the functioning of what Nietzsche calls the "herd." The "herd" is Nietzsche's term for the masses of people who are weak in will and intellect. They constitute the majority of humans and they construct the social order for safety and security. Morality has largely been constructed to protect the herd, as the majority exercises its power to create the conditions for its own defense.[56] Such forces shape the political landscape.

Morality and religion are the vehicles by which control and domination can be exercised over the members of the social order. This is carried out through social conditioning and constant repetition. Thus, the human being can be shaped by social forces over time, as they manifest themselves "in the form of legislation, religions, and customs."[57]

But there is another mechanism that is operating at a cultural level that conveys the need for the state and its corresponding social institutions. With the death of God, where do the masses seek comfort and safety? Nietzsche rejects the argument of Enlightenment humanism that proposes that people are relatively equal in the ability to will, create, and reason. Enlightenment humanism is the moral code of the herd as it has seized control of the political institutions through the process of democratic practice.

In addressing the power of language and culture, and its transformation in the modern period, Nietzsche provides a materialist explanation for the rise of the modern institutional order, specifically the nation-state. In a speech delivered by Zarathustra in Book I, Nietzsche conveys a genealogical under-standing of the modern state. Contrary to liberalism, which identifies the rise of the modern state as the result of human reason applied to the problem of social interactions, Nietzsche suggests a macro-level theory of the psycho-logical conditions that give rise to the state.

Nietzsche has no affection for the state. Nietzsche argues that rule by the herd constitutes a degeneration of culture, but that is not the only reason for his feelings about the state. The state is "the coldest of all cold monsters."[58] Patriotism is described as "fatherlandishness," irrational "soil addiction."[59] It is "insanity."[60] Nationalism is a swindle perpetrated by politicians.[61] It is a "fiction," something that has been constructed.[62]

How did the conditions that allowed for the rise of the state come about? A clue to Nietzsche's position comes in the speech, "Of the New Idol." With the death of God, many had lost their way. Religion had given people pur-pose and grounded their morality. The state emerges as "the new idol" and gives them something new to believe in. "'There is nothing greater on earth than I, the regulating finger of God'—thus the monster bellows."[63] Even for those who rejected religion, the state now provides them a new home.[64] The fervor that was once exclusively the domain of religious dedication now is transferred to the state. The state tells them who to love or hate, what is true and what is false.

Therefore, the liberal tradition's account of the rise of the nation-state conveys a misreading of its origins. It also misreads the sequence between the origins of the state and the construction of citizens. There is no sequence of DNA that conveys national identity. Citizens are created, constructed out of the sentiments and interests of the ruling elites. In the democratic age, that means the masses, the herd.

Human beings are shaped by the totality of forces present in the culture. The beliefs and attitudes found among the masses translate into a system of laws, customs, and ritualized behavior. This is precisely how the "slave morality" of Christianity has spread its ideals of guilt, blame, and impotence through the totality of Western culture. It has defined those values as synony-mous with civilization.[65]

Nietzsche is telling us that beliefs and values, as well as the physical environment, have material force in history. Human beings are embedded within a social context that conditions their behavior. He rejects the ideas of transcendent thought and free will, which have been treated in the history of philosophy and religion as the sources of freedom, creativity, and con-science. What remains is a view of human beings as historical creatures possessing drives and instincts which they mask with terms like the "categor-ical imperative," "natural law," and "rationality."

But the force of history and culture does not have a center. It is filled with lies and deceit, but it is less a conspiracy than a long chain of illusions that are increasingly at odds with science, evolutionary theory, and a *natural* understanding of human beings. To Nietzsche, such an outcome is to be expected in a society of unequals.[66] Democracy produces politics of the lowest common denominator. It does not produce a society that ascends.

This is why Nietzsche came to believe that we were heading into a new dark age. The masses have constructed a web of lies in order to make the present appear rational. When the lies all collapse, the masses will have nothing to hold on to. With God and the state revealed as elaborate hoaxes, the purposelessness of existence becomes an overpowering force upon a mass that lacks the ability to create its own meaning in the world. Zarathustra's task is to both tear off the mask of successive illusions and to prepare human beings to take control over their own destinies.

ANALYSIS OF NIETZSCHE'S MATERIALISM

In epistemological terms, Nietzsche appears as a very consistent materialist. He rejects the idea of transcendent truths, not only in the moral realm, but also with regard to our understanding of social phenomena and science. All is an interpretation. All is anthropomorphic. The value of our understanding is in its utility, not in its correspondence with something that is fixed and universal. Nietzsche is, in many ways, setting the stage for some of the materialist discourse on truth that will come after him. Such a position represents an epistemological relativism that emerges with Feyerabend, the poststructuralists, and Althusser in the twentieth century.

Nietzsche's materialist credentials are also supported by the rejection of historical teleologies and his rejection of "purpose" as part of the human discourse. This is what Michel Foucault calls "positive nihilism," and it denies all such claims as social inventions generated out of vanity and pride. Further, we need to read those characterizations as symptoms of decadence and decay. Only a society that has separated itself off from the biological nature of existence could invent such fictions.

Therefore, from a Nietzschean perspective, there must be material forces that direct the character and direction of social change. Our language schemes empower different modes of existence. The world is filled with a variety of social modes, gods, and narratives on subjectivity. What selects among them is not their *truth* or their consistencies with some historical dynamic. The movement from one mode of existence to another is manifested by the differing amounts of power among competing groups in the larger arena of social forces.

It is not possible to pronounce the *right way* in history. Understanding, critique, and analysis do not have an objective standing. There is no neutral ground on which to stand to make objective analysis. Such a position is echoed by Jacques Derrida in the middle of the twentieth century. There is only the completion among competing narratives of social existence the force each generates for itself.

Some narratives may be better than others. Some may better serve our survival, growth, and development. Some may give us greater latitude for our creativity. Scientific culture is superior to medievalism. But that does mean that our direction as a culture cannot be altered. The Enlightenment belief that reason will generate infinite progress within the future of humanity is relegated to faith rather than fact. There is no guarantee that force of religious culture cannot once again emerge and set the pattern for social and political life. It depends on the relative strength of each mode of existence within the political landscape. To Nietzsche, the reality is that every mode of existence will define reason in a way that makes its activities appear as rational to itself. All our anthropomorphisms feed upon themselves in the end.

Genealogical analysis reveals the material influence of beliefs and ideas. Nietzsche's point is that it is not truth but power that drives the direction of social change. It is not our correctness that dictates history, but the array of forces that emerges from the material conditions of social existence. Thus, it is possible for a group like the working class, the bourgeoisie, or religious groups to manifest historical and social changes. However, this does not represent any sort of fixed, eternal definition of justice, but is simply the manifestation of the group's ability to manifest a level of power at a given stage in history. This is the point Nietzsche is trying to make in the *Genealogy of Morals*. Each group will generate its own narrative on what constitutes justice and it will become part of its discourse on subjectivity.

This construction would include a description of the dynamics of historical change that chart the direction of history in a way consistent with the dominant group's rise to power. As new groups and interests become dominant, they will alter the narratives on morality, social institutions, and even the purpose of life itself. They will make their ascendance appear *rational*, as a kind of natural teleological development within social evolution. The content of these changes are, in a sense, epiphenomenal. They are the surface residue of the movement of forces within the material conditions of existence.

Thus, in addition to Nietzsche's ethical and epistemological relativism, there is also a deep level of social and cultural relativism. The point is not that all modes of existence are "good." It's that all modes of existence have the possibility to rise, given the right conditions, and that each has the mechanism to justify itself through the construction of its rationalizing narrative.

To Nietzsche, only a genealogical analysis can reveal the relativistic nature of such claims.

Today it is the force of the scientific method that has emerged as the centerpiece of the narrative on truth. Such was not always the case.

> It is not the victory of science that distinguishes our nineteenth century, but the victory of the scientific method over science . . . All the methods, all the presuppositions of our contemporary science were for millennia regarded with the profoundest contempt; on their account one was excluded from the society of respectable people—one was considered as an "enemy of God," as a reviler of the highest ideal, as "possessed."[67]

Science is providing us with information on how to adjust nature to our needs. It is a method, a means to the tasks that human beings put before it. It is not a mode of existence, but a means to empower one. "Science—the transformation of nature into concepts for the purpose of mastering nature— belongs under the rubric 'means.'"[68]

But science is not only providing interpretations of the regularity of the world and its inanimate elements. It is also providing a foundation for a new understanding of human beings. The inductive logic employed by Darwin is not only placing human beings back among the animals. It is also providing the basis for an evolutionary understanding of human ontology. Darwin gives a scientific foundation of the notion of "becoming."

But to Nietzsche, even science must be put in its place. Science provides only a "relative rightness" about the world. Its knowledge is human-centric. It represents a structure for generating knowledge that is relative to human beings. The thing-in-itself remains allusive.

Even though Nietzsche rejects both Hegelianism and dialectics, he accepts the notion that history and culture are dynamic. Shifting the discourse from "being" to "becoming" is very important in Nietzsche's general framework.

> The belief that the world as it ought to be is, reality exists, is a belief of the unproductive who do not desire to create a new world as it ought to be. They posit it as already available, they seek ways and means to reach it. "Will to truth"—as the impotence of the will to create.[69]

Such an approach is for a lazy person, "a kind weary of life."[70]

> I seek a conception of the world that takes this fact [becoming] into account. Becoming must be explained without recourse to final intentions; becoming must appear justified at every moment . . . Becoming does not aim at a final state, does not flow into "being" . . . Becoming is an equivalent value every moment; the sum of its values always remains the same; in other words, it has

no value at all, for anything against which to measure it, and in relation to
which the word "value" would have meaning is lacking. [71]

Nietzsche's commitment is clear: "becoming" must be considered without a
teleological endpoint or goal; "becoming" without a means to assign value to
its character; life as transformation. It is hard to imagine such a position
without evolutionary biology.

But this raises an interesting question. To what degree does a firm commitment to indeterminism, chance, relativism, and an opposition to "being"
constitute such a firm ontological position that it undermines the materialist
character of Nietzsche agenda. Or, on the other hand, is this to be understood
as the only ontological position that can stand within a materialist framework. In the final analysis, this may be a distinction without a difference, one
of those philosophic quandaries that result from the structure of classical
philosophic discourse that must give way.

"Becoming" puts everything in flux. Science is only interpretive. Evolution implies constant adaptation and change. The thing-in-itself is revealed as
the illusion, the allusive "being" under the reality of "becoming." In such an
environment there is no possibility to identify "being," and hence, no possibility to create fixed and stable structures as either concepts or the institutional order.

Nietzsche asserts a kind of meta-ontological position, one that denies the
possibility of generating fixed ontological content. There is only change and
beings that are affected by all the conditions that give rise to it. These beings
possess drives and instincts identified as the "will to power," a term given to
the force of adaptation and change that is part of our becoming. It is primordial being outside the repression and sublimation of the *rationality project* in
the Western world.

Even the notion of the "will to power" does not characterize "being" but
seeks to explain processes. To say that life is defined by the will to power is a
characterization not of being but of the activity that defines what it means to
have "life." But this is not vitalism. Nietzsche asserts no notions of life force
that has existence outside the organism. What we call consciousness, or
mind, is simply that mechanism by which the body adjusts to the understanding of its materiality both as needs and as the finitude of existence.

In typical sardonic fashion, Nietzsche mocks the futility of all our apollonian constructions. "Man has gradually become a visionary animal, who has
to fulfil one more condition of existence than the other animals; man must
from time to time believe that he knows *why* he exists; his species cannot
flourish without periodically confiding in life! Without the belief in *reason in
life!*" [72]

It is life as a "role of the dice." There is no grand purpose, only beings
trying to get along, relying on some interpretive understanding of them-

selves, others, and their surroundings as a necessary means of survival. Everything else is illusion.

From Plato to Kant, human beings have implicitly been told that they must repress their instincts to build civilization. Anticipating Freud, Nietzsche fears the results of such repression. Instincts and passion are part of our nature.

Does this constitute a hard ontological position? Perhaps more than is consistent with the parameters of strict materialism. However, it should be noted that in many respects Nietzsche is actually trying to describe "life" rather than "being." It would also be hard to deny the influence of German romanticism on his sentiments.

CONCLUSION

Nietzsche will set the stage for much of the philosophic discourse in the twentieth century. He both critiques and absorbs elements in the Western tradition, engaging Kant, Schopenhauer, Spinoza, Plato, and others. He takes the skeptical elements in Kant and develops them into an epistemological doctrine. To Nietzsche, Kant's genius was to show the limitations of science and logic.[73] Nietzsche also challenges the assumptions of the Kantian ethical system. It was always Nietzsche's position that we must take the world as it is given to us, rather than create an illusion of how we would like it to be. To enact a known falsehood is to set course on the road to nihilism.

He rejects the dialectic methods of Hegel and Marx, denying that their deterministic and teleological elements can provide useful information to the study of human history. They have a subjective, wishful character about them. In the case of Hegel, human beings appear as a kind of epiphenomenon, an afterthought for a reified notion of the transcendent. In the case of Marx and socialism, it represents neither truth nor history, but the desires of the most stupid form of herd animal. Socialism has also not given up on the idea of good and evil, something essential to a Nietzschean analysis of society.[74] It has simply recast the villains.

Weber's relationship with Nietzsche is more complex. Weber lived a generation after Nietzsche and had familiarity with Nietzsche's writings. Nietzsche had gained notoriety by the end of the nineteenth century and Weber had read his work. Nietzsche is mentioned numerous times, particularly in Weber's later essays. Weber refers to the *Genealogy* as a "brilliant essay."[75] He references Nietzsche's concept of the "last men," echoing the claim that it is naïve to believe that science can answer the questions of human happiness or how we should live.[76]

Yet, despite the admiration, Weber could not be considered a Nietzschean. Weber's distinction of facts and values is too artificial, too Kantian, for it to be compatible with Nietzsche's framework. Weber does not relativize and anthropomorphize the Western "rationality project" the way Nietzsche does. To Weber, science still has an objective character about it that the other avenues of inquiry should emulate. That is not what Nietzsche has in mind.

Where there is some "meeting of the minds" is on the subjective character of values. Weber, like Nietzsche, rejects the idea that science can provide human beings with values. Further, they both reject the idea that values can be the result of some transcendent process of reason. In this sense, they both are moving the study of human society in a more materialistic direction.

Regarding empiricism, Nietzsche's criticisms are not dissimilar to those of Marx. Empiricism is too "mechanical."[77] It does not deal with the question of life. Instead it treats human activity as the movement of atoms and molecules. Such explanations cannot address the complexity of social growth and evolution.

Everyone since Nietzsche has to come to terms with his position, one way or the other. A large measure of its appeal is its materialistic character. He manages to combine Darwin's evolutionary theory with a presentation of what he believes Darwin means for our understanding of philosophy, society, and politics. Evolutionary biology means that we cannot treat human nature as static and fixed. It means that science, as well as society, must be understood as an interpretive means for human survival. All our institutional creations must be comprehended in relation to their material origins and the material conditions that maintain their functions. Such breadth makes this a powerful method for generating a materialist understanding of our relationship to the experience and maintenance of life.

NOTES

1. Friedrich Nietzsche, "Joyful Wisdom," in *Nietzsche Selections*. Ed. by Richard Schacht (New York: Scribner/Macmillan), 107.

2. Friedrich Nietzsche, "On Truth and Lies in a Nonmoral Sense," in *Nietzsche Selection*, 45.

3. Friedrich Nietzsche, *The Will to Power* (New York: Random House, 1967), 267.

4. Nietzsche, *The Will to Power*, 280.

5. Nietzsche, *The Will to Power*, 263.

6. Nietzsche, *The Will to Power*, 264.

7. Nietzsche, *The Will to Power*, 266.

8. Nietzsche, *The Will to Power*, 298.

9. Nietzsche, "On Truth and Lies," 49.

10. Nietzsche, *The Will to Power*, 266.

11. Friedrich Nietzsche, *Beyond Good and Evil* (New York: Vintage, 1966), 21.

12. Nietzsche, "On Truth and Lies," 50.

13. Nietzsche, "On Truth and Lies," 51-52.

14. Nietzsche, "On Truth and Lies," 51.

15. Nietzsche, *The Will to Power*, 459.

16. Nietzsche, *The Will to Power*, 267.

17. Gilles Deleuze, *Nietzsche and Philosophy* (New York: Columbia University Press, 1983), 2.

18. Friedrich Nietzsche, *On the Genealogy of Morals and Ecce Homo* (New York: Vintage, 1967), 29-31.

19. Nietzsche, "Joyful Wisdom," 116-117.

20. Nietzsche, *Beyond Good and Evil*, 98.

21. Friedrich Nietzsche, "Twilight of the Idols," in *Nietzsche Selections*, 315.

22. Nietzsche, *Beyond Good and Evil*, 99.

23. Nietzsche, *Beyond Good and Evil*, 99.

24. Nietzsche, *The Will to Power*, 267.

25. Nietzsche, *The Genealogy of Morals*, 45.

26. Nietzsche, "Joyful Wisdom," 314, and "The Antichrist." in *The Portable Nietzsche* (New York: Viking Press, 1968), 598.

27. Nietzsche, "The Antichrist," 580.

28. Nietzsche, *Beyond Good and Evil*, 48.

29. Nietzsche, *The Will to Power*, 148.

30. Nietzsche, *Beyond Good and Evil*, 48.

31. Nietzsche, *The Will to Power*, 407.

32. Friedrich Nietzsche, *The Gay Science* (New York: Vintage, 1974), 261.

33. Nietzsche, "The Antichrist," 580, also *Beyond Good and Evil*, 28.

34. Nietzsche, *The Gay Science*, 262.

35. Nietzsche, "Twilight of the Idols," 311.

36. Nietzsche, *The Will to Power*, 340.

37. Nietzsche, *The Will to Power*, 340.

38. Nietzsche, *The Will to Power*, 3.

39. Nietzsche, *The Will to Power*, 503.

40. Nietzsche, "Twilight of the Idols," 310.

41. Nietzsche, *The Genealogy of Morals*, 62.

42. Nietzsche, *The Will to Power*, 519.

43. Nietzsche, *The Will to Power*, 501.

44. Nietzsche, *The Will to Power*, 272.

45. Nietzsche, "The Antichrist," 579.

46. Nietzsche, *The Will to Power*, 315.

47. Nietzsche, "Twilight of the Idols," 315.

48. Nietzsche, "The Antichrist," 570.

49. Nietzsche, "The Antichrist," 570.

50. Nietzsche, "On Truth and Lies," 47.

51. Nietzsche, *The Will to Power*, 275.

52. Nietzsche, "On Truth and Lies," 48.

53. Nietzsche, *The Will to Power*, 283.

54. Nietzsche, *The Will to Power*, 283.

55. Nietzsche, "On Truth and Lies," 51.

56. Nietzsche, *The Genealogy of Morals*, 46.

57. Nietzsche, *The Will to Power*, 93.

58. Friedrich Nietzsche, *Thus Spoke Zarathustra* (Middlesex, England: Penguin Books, 1971), 75.

59. Nietzsche, *Beyond Good and Evil*, 174

60. Nietzsche, *Beyond Good and Evil*, 196.

61. Nietzsche, *The Will to Power*, 49.

62. Nietzsche, *Beyond Good and Evil*, 188.

63. Nietzsche, *Thus Spoke Zarathustra*, 76.

64. Nietzsche, *Thus Spoke Zarathustra*, 76.

65. Nietzsche, *The Genealogy of Morals*, 42-43.

66. Nietzsche, *The Will to Power*, 397.

67. Nietzsche, *The Will to Power*, 261.

68. Nietzsche, *The Will to Power*, 328.

69. Nietzsche, *The Will to Power*, 317.

70. Nietzsche, *The Will to Power*, 317.

71. Nietzsche, *The Will to Power*, 377 – 378.

72. Nietzsche, "Joyful Wisdom," 103.

73. Friedrich Nietzsche, *The Birth of Tragedy and the Genealogy of Morals* (Garden City, NY: Doubleday, 1956), 111.

74. Nietzsche, *The Will to Power*, 19.

75. Max Weber, "The Social Psychology of World Religions," in *From Max Weber* (New York: Oxford University Press: 1946), 270.

76. Max Weber, "Science as a Vocation," in *From Max Weber*, 143.

77. Nietzsche, *The Genealogy of Morals*, 24.

Chapter Six

Poststructuralism and the
Material Force of Text

INTRODUCTION

Poststructuralism emerges in the twentieth century as an intellectual movement that encompasses many of the ideas already discussed in this work and
seeks to draw these materialist threads together into a coherent perspective.
Poststructuralism adopts the Kantian idea that our descriptions of the world
cannot address the questions of *essence* and remain epistemologically sound.
The influence of Marx is complex and multifaceted. Marx is identified as
setting the realm of social inquiry in an overtly materialist direction, but is
also criticized for slips into essentialist language and historical universals.
From Weber, there is the concern with *rationalization* in the West, and the
way in which that process has set the direction of both the political order and
the condition of subjectivity. This is of particular interest to Jean Baudrillard
and his work on simulation. Finally, there is Friedrich Nietzsche. It would be
hard to overstate Nietzsche's influence as it shapes twentieth-century thought
directly and through the incorporation of some of his ideas in the works of
others.

This chapter will employ a simple strategy. I will assume the epistemological challenge to *essence* is already "baked in" to this line of inquiry.
Therefore, the work will begin with a summary and reinterpretation of the
Marxian project. This will be augmented with some challenges to Marx's
general assumptions by Louis Althusser. The critique of Marx will be used as
a bridge over to the work of Jean Baudrillard and the significance of simulation as a manifestation of epistemological relativism. The focus will then
shift to Jacques Derrida and the technology of dissemination. Then the chap-

ter will move to a discussion of Michel Foucault on the construction of subjectivity and its connection to the exercise of power.

Like the preceding chapters, the last section will address the extent to which poststructuralism can be said to meet the conditions of a coherent materialist doctrine outlined in chapter 1. In order to address the extent to which poststructuralism can be construed as a materialist doctrine, several issues must be confronted. If, as poststructuralism argues, "text" is everything, how is this compatible with the general assumptions of materialism? Materialism is premised on the idea of an *external* reality that imposes itself on human beings. To what extent does "text" fulfill that condition?

There is also the question of domain. Is materialism a doctrine that has as its domain physics, biology, philosophy, or society more generally? Some field of discourse must be established in order to make the materialism coherent. This question can also not be separated from the questions regarding the influence of history and "context" in the discussion of materialism.

In addition, there are the issues surrounding the relationship between materialism and consciousness. What is determinant in the formation of thoughts and ideas? Materialism, generally, has been associated with the notion that consciousness is not independent of the world. Consciousness, and the ideas that constitute an understanding of *reality*, has its origin in the influence of external conditions. This is the case whether consciousness is viewed as the manifestation of raw sensation, the result of physical adaptation, or as the result of historical forces.

Therefore, the question of materiality is also a question of what moves history. What forces direct the behavior of human actors? There is also the question of sequence among ideas, the environment, and actions.

If we act according to the picture of reality that we consider accurate, then it is necessary to ask about the origin of that image. If idealism and all forms of transcendentalism are rejected, then the sequence must begin with experience, broadly defined. Experience of physical sensation and experience of cultural context cannot be considered either mutually exclusive or hierarchically arranged. Context provides sensation with meaning. The text on reality is both the origin and the outcome of a process of social reproduction.

Institutional power reflects and reinforces the cultural patterns, norms, and practices of any given society. Thrasymachus speaks of such a process in Plato's *Republic*.[1] The text directs human activity. It has material force, even without material extension.

Such a position cannot be developed outside of a radical relativism. However, this is not the well-worn path of ethical relativism that remains part of the modernist discourse. What Thrasymachus, Nietzsche, Derrida, Foucault, and other poststructuralists suggest is an epistemological relativism that asserts the anthropomorphic character of knowledge itself. If this is the case, then human beings create a human-centered knowledge that is circulated in the process of historical change.

MARX, ENGELS, AND THE
LIMITATIONS OF HISTORICAL MATERIALISM

The Marxian formulation of materialism has many facets. It is a formulation of materialist doctrine that emerges in the wake of Hegelian philosophy and Darwin's evolutionary biology. It articulates a circumscribed, yet profound, notion of socio-cultural reproduction. However, the Marxian argument also lapses, at times, into essentialist and teleological claims that violate the more materialist components of its premises.

The Material Origins of Subjectivity

Central to understanding this form of materialism is the significance of biology. Marx and Engels refer to Darwin and evolutionary biology as the central component in modern materialism. There is a conscious rejection of the empirical form of materialism. The movement of particles is insufficient to explain the functioning of human society. History must be understood as the product of living beings, not the random collisions of inanimate objects. Thus, biological necessity is the origin of human activity. The organism must interact with the natural environment in order to gather the necessities of material existence. Consciousness is shaped by this experience of actual life processes.[2]

From this perspective, the "material origins of consciousness" has a double meaning. The material existence of human beings is a necessary condition for the possibility of human thought and consciousness. Marx denies the epistemological basis for Hegelian idealism and other forms of transcendentalist speculation. But further, in identifying the source for the content of consciousness, Marx also asserted material origins to the thoughts and ideas of consciousness itself. Human materiality leads to biological necessity. Biological necessity drives human production. In the process of production, we generate the ideas of who and what we are in the unfolding of history. Consciousness is, therefore, a social product.[3]

If our materiality forces the interaction with nature, and this interaction is the basis of our thoughts and ideas, then it shapes both our understanding of ourselves as subjects in the world and dictates the institutional structures we create on the basis of that understanding. Ideas, social structures, institutional practices, and politics are a necessary reflection of the materiality of existence. As human interaction with nature is conditioned by experience, there can be no fixed human nature, and no fixed understanding of morality.[4] In short, human subjectivity is constructed historically.

Human history is the history of the development of human productive capacities.[5]

It is a law of history in which all impediments to the increasing productivity of labor will be broken down.[6] Production is the base on which the entire superstructure of human association is constructed. Since Marx asserts that the form of productive activity, the *mode of production*, determines the ideas and institutions in a given historical period, the economic sphere is given the position as the determining factor in the course and direction of historical change. In Marx's terminology, the *mode of production* determines the *relations of production*.[7]

Revolutionary changes in human association have been tied to these material premises. Changes in the mode of production have necessitated changes in the political and social institutions that govern society. The relations of production have been altered as human beings have developed from hunter-gatherers, to agricultural producers, into the industrial mode of production. Capitalism, as a set of social arrangements, arises with the early phase of industrialization. As capital consolidates, and as monopoly production replaces competition, capitalism becomes an impediment to the further development of human productive capacities.[8] The internal logic of capitalism, the impoverishment of labor, the tension between labor and machine production, are all part of an economic logic that generates the need for a new form in the relations of production.

However, capitalism is not just an economic system to Marx. It is also a system of oppression. Capitalism is based on the extraction of *surplus value* from the workforce. Simply stated, surplus value is the amount of value produced by the workers beyond the amount for which they are paid. Since wages are determined by supply and demand, it is possible to produce value beyond the value that is transferred as a wage. This value, "smiles upon the capitalist with all the charms of an entity created out of nothing."[9]

Problems with the Marxian Formulation

What is striking about the criticisms of Marx and Marx's methodology is the similarity regarding the general themes in the critiques. This is the case even among those who are sympathetic to the objectives of the Marxian project and those who offer praise to Marx's accomplishments.

Louis Althusser is an important figure in the attempt to broaden Marx's methodological strategy. Althusser is influenced by the Marxian tradition and is often identified as a structural Marxist. He is committed to the general character of Marx's analysis, the emphasis on a materialist understanding of history and the structures of capitalist power, but Althusser is also influenced by the critiques of metaphysics and essentialist characterization of the subject that are more reflective of poststructuralism.

For Althusser, the assertion that the economic base is always decisive in the formation of consciousness is simply too narrow and deterministic. As a result, the distinction between base and superstructure that Marx presented cannot be sustained. Base and superstructure are both part of the materiality of contextual conditions that will shape the consciousness of individuals. [10]

Another criticism is offered by Max Weber, Jean Baudrillard, and Jacques Derrida. This has to do with Marx's epistemological claims regarding the status of his historical analysis. As Weber puts it, all Marxian laws of history are actually "ideal-types."[11] What Weber means by this is that Marx has presented an interpretive model of history based on selected indicators. It cannot be conceived as the truth of history itself. Baudrillard makes a similar claim, arguing that Marx made a mistake in presenting his hypothesis as a universal movement of history. To Baudrillard, such an assertion has a meta-physical character. [12] A similar point is made by Jacques Derrida in *Positions*, contending that Marx falsely attempts to escape charges of metaphysical speculation by resting his assertions on a teleological conception of history. [13]

Another problem stems from the essentialist foundation used to support Marx's normative claims regarding capitalism. Marxism blends elements of biological and socio-cultural materialism, but the relativism embodied in these doctrines is undercut by the discussion of human nature that supports a normative critique of capitalist practice. In the early Marx, such as *The 1844 Manuscripts*, the normative critique of capitalism emerges from an essential-ist ontology, which asserts a *natural* condition of human nature that is altered by capitalist social relations. [14] Estrangement means separation, alienation from a condition that is professed to be essential to human nature. Such an essentialist claim contradicts the historical relativity that is part of Marxian materialism.

The point here is not to bash Marx, but to echo the point made by Derrida. Marx is an opening, not an end. He provides a path rather than a finished product. [15]

Poststructuralism and the Cultural Determination of Consciousness

Marx's analysis of the inner logic of capitalism is quite profound. However, the economic determinism that is asserted in the relationship between base and superstructure cannot be sustained. Other forms of oppression manifest themselves in society that do not have their origins in class. Discrimination based on gender, sexual orientation, national identity, and religious or non-religious sentiments have their origins in a process that can be connected to economic production only through the most thread-bare type of analysis. Prejudice in these areas must be linked to a more general consideration of social reproduction.

Within this alternative framework, a new understanding of power must be formulated. From the poststructuralist perspective, power resides in every institutional structure that has the ability to define what constitutes the content of subjectivity. This means that every institution within society must have an internal process in which it transmits and enforces the ideas and practices that underpin the institution's existence. There is no meta-logic that animates social reproduction, but each norm must find its own equilibrium within the general processes of society. For this reason, it is possible for ideas and practices to change within one subsystem without a complete alteration of the domain of social reproduction.

Logically, materialism does not allow the process to be driven by a historical teleology or even a notion of necessary historical progress. Change is simply change. It occurs when the pattern of subjectivity has been altered in an area of identity formation. Judgments regarding the normative value of one direction over another can only be made from within the structures themselves and do not possess an external form of validation.

Ideas move history. However, this is not to make a claim associated with nineteenth-century idealism. Ideas are not the product of transcendent processes. They do not have an existence outside of the lived historical experience of human beings. Ideas have material origins in the totality of our experiences. The source of our ideas is the processes that exist for the reproduction of the conditions of our material existence, which includes our social and cultural experiences. Thus, the ideas that move history are the manifestation of the material processes of social reproduction.

Althusser and the Material Power of Ideology

Concern for the means by which people construct their identity is a major focus of the work by Louis Althusser. Althusser is influenced by Marx, thus he is concerned with capitalism and the oppressive nature of capitalist society. But Althusser's project is animated by assumptions regarding epistemology and the nature of our reality that move him closer to the definition of materialism outlined in chapter 1.

For Althusser, what we consider to be social reality is actually a symbolic construction. This symbolic construction takes place at the level of cognition. It is based on the information we process from the totality of social conditions. Thus, we are constantly encountering symbolic messages regarding identity, normative behavior, social practices and structures that are asserted to be *true* or *real* but are, in fact, the ideas and beliefs that serve to regenerate the existing order of society. *Reality* is the true "*ding an sich*" that remains, in its essence, forever hidden from us.

In place of reality we have ideology. Ideology is the symbolic language that we absorb from our social interaction and which informs our actions. It shapes our thinking about who we are and how we should behave. It creates a set of foundational principles upon which we construct our understanding of both the material reproduction and the system by which we order and classify our knowledge about our experiences.[16] Ideology is embedded in all our practices and structures.

The materiality of ideology is in the fact that beliefs push human history. In defining human beings and the expectations of human existence, ideology represents subjectivity as a set of normative anticipations. At a societal level, these are encoded into law, constitutions, and the structure of social power. Variation from the norms would generate a negative reaction. This will take place within the institutions of power in the society, and would be legitimated by the support of the broader population that has been socialized to institutional norms. Althusser makes this point in outlining the importance of a mechanism for maintaining the legitimacy of structural hierarchies and the system of capitalist production. He calls this the *ideological state apparatus*.

For Althusser, capitalism requires a legitimating discourse. It has in place a system of rewards and punishments that are embedded within its institutional practices. Capital controls the military, the police, and the generation of laws and policies that support the status quo. It is Althusser's point that capitalism also uses a complex system of social institutions that reinforce the ideological conditions that further the beliefs that make capitalist practice rational. There is an inverse relationship between systemic levels of legitimacy (as a *belief* in the naturalness of the institutional order) and the need for the exercise of force to maintain system stability. Both state and non-state institutions participate.

> An Ideological State Apparatus is a system of defined institutions, organizations, and the corresponding practice. Realized in the institutions, organization, and practices of this system is all or part (generally speaking, a typical combination of certain elements) of the State Ideology. This ideology realized in an ISA ensures its systemic unity on the basis of an 'anchoring" in the material functions specific to each ISA; these function are not reducible to the ideology, but serve it as "support."[17]

The ideological state apparatus includes schools, media, publishing houses, cultural outlets, churches, and families. They create the symbolic image of what constitutes societal norms. In doing so, they construct a narrative regarding the rationality of societal power structures.

The content of the ideology is distinctive from its structures. However, Althusser makes it clear that ideological content does not form in a vacuum. He states that there is no such thing as "spontaneous content."[18] The content will serve the existing power structure in society.

Louis Althusser is a significant figure in restructuring the underlying assumptions of Marxian epistemology. He undercuts the Marxian claims that reference "reality" and "human essence" by eliminating the concept of the *real* in our understanding of history and society. The *real* is treated as a symbolic, linguistic construction. Our cognitions are shaped by the belief we have in the *real* rather than the *real* itself. Nevertheless, Althusser remains a transitional figure, still focused heavily on production and the sovereignty of the state.

Baudrillard: The End of the Real

Of all the writers that generally fall under the domain of poststructuralism, none is more focused on the question of the *real* than Jean Baudrillard. Baudrillard argues that today it is impossible to identify a true reality.[19] Our experience of the external world takes place within a cognitive framework that is a constructed abstraction. We do not experience reality, but pass our experiences through a filter that orders those raw experiences into coherence. What we then experience as real is a symbolic reality that is manifested in, and reinforced by, the processes of production and reproduction. What is real takes on the ontological characteristics of what can be generated and transmitted. What is real is what can be disseminated.

What Baudrillard is trying to explore are the mechanisms by which human beings come to understand the *truth* of their reality. That means that he is looking for the material causes of historical transformations in the ways in which human beings have come to see themselves and the means by which they identify the *proper* ordering of social life. We are born into a symbolic order, an order of values and hierarchies, that we did not create but come to reflect as parts of the historical processes that transform over time. This order creates a filter that shapes our definition of what constitutes reality.

If this filter consisted of human faculties for cognition, Baudrillard would be following the lead of Kant. However, Baudrillard is suggesting that these filters are themselves products of historical and cultural conditions. They are reflections of the material conditions of existence. In "The Orders of Simulacra," Baudrillard outlines the historical development that have led to the disconnect between the real and our perception of it.

Baudrillard argues that in feudal times there was a connection between the real and the sign used to designate its reality. With the coming of the Renaissance this order changed. The Renaissance was characterized by a proliferation of images, signs, and symbols in which the notion of the real was increasingly *represented* in objects that stand in for the real. Baudrillard calls this the counterfeit stage, as the representation stood in as a symbolic referent for what it was to convey.[20] Baudrillard claims this period was exemplified by the use of stucco.

The next phase in the development of the simulacra was the industrial order. This phase in history is characterized by production and reproduction.

The key factor here was the possibility of producing mass quantities of identical products. Value was generated out of those products that could be reproduced on a large scale, thus contributing to the massification of culture more generally. This includes the development of mass forms of political organizations and democracy.[21] The equality of consumption helped bring about a general sense of social equality. The prospects for liberation could be found in the contrast between the worker and the bourgeoisie.

In the twentieth century, conditions changed and society moved toward *simulation proper*. This stage is characterized by two phenomena: digital communication and advances in DNA. Together they constitute what Baudrillard refers to as "the code." As he puts it, "Digitality is its metaphysic principle . . . and DNA is its prophet."[22] Binary code is now the condition necessary for communication. DNA will be the source of our knowledge about the human subject. The code creates the illusion of foundational knowledge as it appears to close the gap between the real and the illusory. It presents itself as the real, the source of our knowledge and understanding.[23]

In his later work Baudrillard talks about a fractal stage and the idea of simulation being replaced with the idea of networks,[24] but these ideas can be understood as further refinements of the general logic of simulation. The code is the truth from which society is to be ordered. It creates a self-referencing system from which there is no escape. All human beings are brought under its power. Its logic is circular and closed. For Baudrillard this gives it a totalitarian character.[25]

What was real became symbolic, only to take the form of the real again. However, now the real is only real in relation to the symbolic order which it represents. Simulation has come full circle and folded back in on itself. Today there are no points of reference for the real.[26] There is only simulation.

Baudrillard's work is both provocative and interesting. He provides a materialist reading of causality in history and explores the materiality of power and social change. The end of the real is part of a historical process in which complexes of factors are identified for their causal influences on the dynamics of social and political change.

It is hard to read Baudrillard and not see the influence of Nietzsche. This influence has several facets. Baudrillard gives a negative interpretation to the influences of evolutionary biology in contrast to Nietzsche's more neutral position. But Nietzsche was less pessimistic about the influence of Darwin's ideas. Nietzsche saw evolutionary biology as providing a new path for philosophic exploration. But to Baudrillard there is a danger. To Baudrillard, DNA is simply the vehicle for a new form of technological oppression. DNA can serve as the new foundational principle for fixed and static platforms of social stratification.

Another take on Nietzsche is found in Baudrillard's discussion of illusion. The world is full of illusions. We operate our lives according to these illusions which are embedded and transmitted through the medium of language. For Nietzsche, *Truth* is a movable host of metaphors, metonymies, and anthropomorphisms that have been poetically and rhetorically intensified by usage into fixed truth.[27] In society, truth means using the usual metaphors in the language. The ability to use language is not an expression of truth. It is an expression of power.[28]

Language is always generated from a perspective, expressing the interests of those speaking. For this reason social changes like those associated with a change in values is always representative of a change in the distribution of power in society.[29] Politics is the struggle over whose metaphors will dominate. These claims by Nietzsche leads Gilles Deleuze to conclude that institutions are reactive forces, a training ground for the adaptation to the existing structure of power.[30] To put this in a more general way, the struggles to influence language over matters of race, ethnicity, religion, and class are part of a struggle to control the institutional superstructure that can impose and reinforce the structures of power.

But for Nietzsche the construction of illusion is part of the limitations of the human species and the means by which we cope with a world beyond our comprehension. It is not, therefore, fully negative. It expresses the power and processes of the human mind. It is a tool of survival.

But for Baudrillard, the end of the real is a historical condition rather than an underlying condition of cognition and consciousness. This implies that at some point human beings were connected to the real. In this regard, Nietzsche has the stronger case. We have never grasped the real. The way it is treated in Baudrillard seems to relegate the real to a time prior to cognition. Hence, Baudrillard tends to treat the *real* as a metaphysical category, itself an abstraction, rather than an ever-moving, ungraspable aspiration of human enterprise. It takes on the character of a rhetorical device, never fully lending itself to definition.

Jacques Derrida: The Graft and the Scission in the Material Transmission of Text

The influence of Nietzsche's thoughts on the questions of knowledge and consciousness are clearly evident in the work of Jacques Derrida. Derrida moves away from the metaphysical character of nineteenth- and twentieth-century phenomenology, from Hegel to Heidegger, to a position that is much closer to that of Nietzsche. Husserl and Heidegger are, to Derrida, still engaged in a metaphysical enterprise. Their goal is to define the essence of *being*. Such a project misunderstands the material origins of language and consciousness. In this sense, one way to understand Derrida's project is to frame it in terms of Nietzsche's. Much of Derrida's theoretical discussion of *text* follows from Nietzsche's discussion on the metaphorical nature of language. Derrida explores the significance and implications of such a claim within the context of linguistics.

The intent of Derrida's project is to create a materialist understanding of how human beings generate and transmit their understanding of the world. In doing so, Derrida outlines a description of the means by which the embedded processes of culture found within institutional existence are transformed into elements that move history. Derrida's work is part of the semiotic discourse on the role of the *sign* in the transmission of cultural patterns. What is significant about this discourse is that it takes as one of its premises the idea that the construction and usage of a sign is always a mediated process. The Kantian assertion that experience is mediated by the categories found in the human mind is now reformulated. The mediation of experience for reflection and the creation of texts is directed by the cultural structures that intervene between sensation and cognition.

Derrida claims that all of Western metaphysics is a search for a "transcendental signified."[31] The transcendental significance connotes that something has an existence that is independent of language, but that can simultaneously be represented in language. Language assigns properties to objects as the subject confronts the objective world. As a representation in language, its domain is artificially circumscribed. Such a view is the cornerstone of the Western logocentric position, and is an important assumption underlying the empirically based doctrine of materialism.

However, there is a problem. In order to represent the object, the domain of properties assigned to the object must maintain stability. This means that the list of potential properties must be closed. If the representation is artificially closed for the purpose of ontological stability, it committed an epistemological error. The need to assign *being* has overridden the property of openness. The representation's metaphysical character is secured by this process.

Further, such a process must be characterized as *mediated*, in the sense that the properties assigned to an object must be sorted and selected for their meaning and significance to *being*. What determines the selection of these traits? The significant factor is its connection to a chain of previous texts projecting back through time. Texts are linked to other texts.

If the representation of the external is mediated, both as it is experienced and as it is turned into a sign for transmission, then where is the ground upon which one can stand in order to validate it objectively? Derrida does not claim there is nothing that is real (although he is often falsely accused of that) but simply that there is no discourse that can be engaged about the real that is not metaphysical in character.[32] All objects are mediated by the act of representing. Therefore, all the texts about the real can be deconstructed to reveal their metaphysical character.

Derrida explains an alternative conception of the process of representation in his work, *Dissemination*. The concept of *dissemination* explains a material process of cultural transmission that operates outside the possibility of assigning *essence* to a sign. Signs cannot be divorced from the historical and ideological components that form their content.[33] Deconstruction, claims Derrida, should reveal the artificiality of closure that gives force to ideological constructions.[34] Philosophy cannot achieve closure as to the identity of its objects.[35] Words give the illusion that a stable identity has been assigned.[36] However, such claims are illusory.

Texts refer to other texts. They do not capture the ontological character of *being*. Therefore, culture is the material process of transmitting texts in which the biases and systemic assumptions are passed on in a process of cultural reproduction. Texts do not receive their legitimacy from correspondence to an absolute reality that they claim to have captured. Rather, legitimacy comes from the traces of previous texts found within the newly generated text. Therefore, textual generation represents a process of *grafting*.[37] Such a view voids the possibility of a text having a detectable beginning, raising questions about the modernist notion of assigning ownership of a text to an author. A text is always the transformation of a previous text in an endless and complex cycle of cultural reproduction.[38]

Further, since closure with regard to the identity of objects can be secured only artificially, committing an epistemological error, there must be some mechanism by which ordinary language is operationalized in the conduct of daily life. Text cannot convey the infinite richness of objects and historical processes. There are infinite possibilities and a plurality of contexts. How do we construct meaningful discourse?

Derrida's answer is simple. We "take a cut of it."[39] He calls this a "scission." The scission is a cutout of the infinite possibilities for identities and contextual meanings. The text must be assigned a beginning and an end. Its fullness cannot be represented. Its space must be limited, and it must be assigned closure. Such actions give all texts a mythical character.

The graft and the scission do not have ontological status in the traditional sense. However, the graft and the scission have material force. They shape the society, not in conformity with a "natural reality," but in conformity with the transmitted norms, structures, and expectations that make up its content.

The notion that our ideas about reality are the result of the transmission of experience and ideologies that are part of a process of cultural programming means that the discussion of this process cannot be divorced from the social distribution of power. This explains Derrida's return to Marx in *Specters of Marx*. Derrida seeks to bring the materialist elements of Marx under the umbrella of deconstruction. In this framework, their common agenda is to wage a war against the representation of human essence as it is a mask to cover the interests of power and subjugation. A materialist critique can expose how the assertion of a fixed, stable identity takes the form of an imposition by the forces that control the instruments of dissemination.

However, Derrida seeks to reveal the material nature of this process without assigning determining power exclusively to the realm of economics. The content of culture was born of material premises, the existence of creatures seeking the successful material activity in the world. The texts that they create do not capture the essence of reality but are reflections of ideologies and interests. These texts are transmitted through a material process of cultural reproduction. They result in an effect on the material activity of all that are part of their historical sway.

Foucault, the Plurality of Power, and the Politics of the Material Body

Derrida makes it clear that he sees his conception of deconstruction as a political concept. It is an "intervention."[40] It seeks to disrupt the transmission of the dominant text on subjectivity and reduce it to an ideological construct. It seeks to prevent the homogenizing effect that such a transmission produces. It seeks to prevent the construction of Nietzsche's "last man," a project viewed as the culmination of the modernity project.

From its earliest formulations, modern humanism has sought to create a universal definition of the subject that will serve as a firm foundation upon which to build the structures of institutional existence. In the seventeenth and eighteenth centuries subjectivity was contained within explicit and implicit narratives of Western social life. By the end of the nineteenth and beginning of the twentieth century scientific techniques were introduced in order to bring this project into conformity with the contemporary epistemic models of knowledge.

This *modernity project* has been designed to produce a transcendent, universal notion of subjectivity. This model of the human being can be found in the Enlightenment Humanism that dominated much of the twentieth century. This is, in part, the point that Baudrillard is trying to make with his focus on "the code," as the contemporary totalizing methodology.

Once this meta-narrative on subjectivity has been established political and social life can become dominated by a deductive logic. Human nature takes on the character of a foundational discourse from which the normal course of human activity can be identified. Deviation can also be discerned.

In creating a logic that underlies social and ethical prescriptions, a rationale for the exercise of power is also created. Norms are generated and enforced based on the characteristics assigned in the discourse on subjectivity. Within the discourse, the exercise of power is manifested as authority, a legitimated act of power.

The exercise of power within the discourse on subjectivity is a central concern of Michel Foucault. If we assume that Nietzsche is correct, then the world as we understand it is made up of cognitions that are human-centric in character and tied to our need to survive and thrive in a context that is historical and contingent. All our cognitions have an illusory character. There is simply no way that a totalizing discourse on the human character can be constructed. That is not to say that phenomenal statements regarding human appearances cannot be generated, such as all human beings have ten toes. However, the quest for the narrative on the subject seeks something far deeper. It wants to uncover the *essence* of the human being in order to create an institutional order that reflects that essence.

The poststructuralists generally share the view that institutional discourse is local, historical, and contingent. No such transcendent definition of subjectivity can be constructed. Foucault focuses on the power dimension of this nexus between subjectivity and state sovereignty. The discourse on subjectivity must always be interrogated. If power cannot serve a truth that is not there, it must be asked, "who does it serve?"[41]

This is the materialist question behind Foucault's method of genealogy. If knowledge is constructed using the biases, ideologies, and interests that are present within the institutional structure from which it is generated, then the outcome will always reinforce the norms and practices of a given institution. Truth and power cannot be separated. Truth is in a circular relation with the system of power.[42] It does not reinforce a transcendent claim, but enhances the system of power that was its origins. In every society, discourse is controlled by the structure of power.[43]

Genealogy does not focus on subjectivity, except as an effect of the exercise of power. Genealogy is a method to study the historical exercise of power that does not rely on the existence of the transcendental subject. The subject is seen as the product of institutional practices, not their cause. In this way, Foucault can maintain a commitment to a material understanding of history and still be able to engage in a critique. Critique is carried out by deconstructing the relationship between institutional practices and the metaphysical components in the ideology that support it.

The logic of sovereignty since the time of Plato has been to create an institutional order that, as closely as possible, reflects the natural conditions of human beings. Social harmony is the result of the correspondence between the subjects and the institutional order. In Plato, it is manifested by a political hierarchy that reflects natural inequality. In Hobbes, the institutional logic results from the egoism of human nature. With Kropotkin, there is reason and gregariousness.

Foucault's notion of genealogy reverses the order of the logical relations between subjects and institutions. Institutions are part of the contextual materiality out of which subjectivity is formed. People are born into an institutional order which they did not create. The cues for social action are embedded within the system of rewards and punishments. Therefore, there is a material process in which consciousness is shaped by the interaction between subjects and the institutional order. Subjectivity is constructed, it is not discovered by transcendental reflection. The institutions come first and produce human subjects in their image.

The circular nature of his process, coupled with the general metaphysical character of political ideologies, render this system nontransparent. It is self-referencing, in the sense referred to by Niklas Luhmann.[44] The language of institutions reflects the logic of their existence. This is true of all institutions, whether represented by the church, state, educational, penal, or other. To cite one example, the modern period is characterized by state sovereignty. The nation-state system is not just characterized by territory and domestic political legitimacy. It is also characterized by the creation of characteristics of subjectivity which would be meaningless without the system of nation-state sovereignty. These are concepts such as citizenship, patriotism, and treason. Foucault's point is that such concepts do not have a transcendental character but are products of the particular distribution of power that exists within the historical context of modernity. All institutions create concepts that legitimate their exercise of power.

The power of institutions is manifested as the ability to define human beings as subjects. Power attaches identities to people. In turn, this process ties the individuals to the institutions.[45] By making subjects part of the structure and reinforcing that definition through a system of rewards and punishments, institutions exercise control over human beings and direct their actions in a way that reinforces the logic of the institution itself. As such, subjectivity is viewed as the material product of the contextual relations in which an individual finds itself. There can be no appeal to a transcendent truth of subjectivity from this perspective. Counter-discourses to those that seek to subjugate human beings can be constructed as part of the process in which the metaphysical character of representation is revealed.

Heterogeneity emerges as a normative position as the legitimacy of social homogenization is undermined. *Difference* becomes the basis for counter-narratives on the subject. In the absence of meta-narratives on subjectivity, there is plurality.

For Foucault, even institutional existence is not manifested as a singularity. There is no single institution, such as the state, that controls all aspects of social existence. Modern life is characterized by multiple domains of power, reflecting the plurality of institutional existence. Thus, today subjectivity is pulled in a variety of often competing directions. Medical definitions of the subject differ from those of churches or universities. The emergence of multiple forms of subjectivity becomes the political challenge of the contemporary postmodern order. Women, prisoners, homosexuals, and the proletariat all struggle against the particular form of power and institutions that constrain them.[46] Institutions create a discourse that legitimates the exercise of power. That power is manifested in the control of material bodies.

After constructing definitional content to subjectivity, institutions exercise a claimed *right* to human bodies. This may take the form of a prohibition, as the institutions of state and church have sought to control sexual practices.[47] It may take the form of institutional incarceration, such as in a prison or mental institution.[48] It may create a legal structure to provide access to the capital producing potential of bodies in the production process.[49] It may even conscript bodies in the service of state power. Each institutional *right* is generated out of the institution that exercises that particular power. It can never take the form of a *transcendent right*.

The critique presented by poststructuralist epistemology undermines the efforts that ascribe definitional power to institutions. Foucault reveals the taxonomy of the process of institutional power while denying the validity of any process that seeks to formulate rigid definitions that impose themselves by controlling human bodies. Foucault's point is that with the inability to create an epistemologically sound universal definition of subjectivity, the human experience should be one of self-construction.[50]

What Foucault adds to the discussion of materiality by other poststructuralist authors is a discussion of the relationship between institutional power and the control of human beings. Foucault elaborates not only the arbitrary nature of historical constructions, but also how they function in relation to directing activity. Institutions create self-regenerating discourse. In doing so, they create the conditions for directing the course of human history.

Materialism and Poststructuralist Assumptions

The materialist threads in the continental tradition have moved away from their metaphysical predecessors. With poststructuralism, the Hegelian system's teleology of history is reduced to a creative, yet speculative narrative regarding the nature of human social and political evolution. *Reason* cannot direct history if its content is, itself, a product of that history. Husserl and his followers suffer from the same problem, separating the content of consciousness from the real, concrete experiences of living in the world with the richness of sensual stimulation and social influences.

Collectively, the poststructuralist perspective moves the continental tradition toward a materialist understanding of consciousness. However, this is not a materialism that focuses on strictly the movement of atoms and their impact on the human brain. It is a material understanding of the content of consciousness and cognition. It is a materialism that does not deny the firing of the brain's neurons as part of the materiality of bodies in the world, but one that is also interested in the material processes of experience that become part of human consciousness. These ideas then direct human activity in the world.

Human reason is central to this process, but this reason must be understood within circumscribed limits. What we call reason is subject to the same historical forces as the content of consciousness more generally. What we call reason is, therefore, socially constructed.

This explains why Althusser has difficulty accepting the essentialist element of the Marxian ontology. If the content of reason is socially constructed there is simply no place to stand outside of history and context in order to construct a fixed notion of human essence. This point is clearly articulated by Derrida.

In this sense, poststructuralism is very relativistic. There is heavy emphasis on the social and cultural influences on human consciousness in a context that is continually moving and open to change. History is dynamic and human beings are situated within the historical process.

Central to this understanding is the concept of *change* and its implications. There are the radical ruptures that Foucault discusses, that establish new epistemological rules that govern our understanding of the world. There is also the subtler, yet sublime, process of dissemination discussed by Derrida, in which the ideas and concepts of one generation are passed on to the next through the technology of language. The foundation of knowledge and consciousness, is therefore, its own transmission. If the link between sign and referent is severed, if texts refer only to other texts in a chain of diffusion back through history, there is nothing but text as the foundation of our thinking. There can be nothing called *reason* that is divorced from the context in which it arises.

For this reason, the poststructuralists reject the notion of a fixed view of human nature. They see the epistemological program in Western philosophy as one of trying to create a fixed and firm foundation for human thought and activity. Central to this project has been the attempts to create a definition of subjectivity. From Plato to Marx this project dominated political theory as such a foundation could provide the concrete platform for political prescriptions.

This provides entry into one of the poststructuralist's most important political insights. Human beings are created, not discovered. The *nature* of the human character is a product of the totality of forces to which it is subject. Thus, the totality of the social environment needs to be understood as the determining factor is the structure of human beings. The individual is made in this process.

Some of these determining factors may be more important than others. Production, media, education, and institutional bureaucracies are clearly some of the most important factors when it comes to environmental factors shaping consciousness. However, what is important is always subject to change. Religious institutions still hold some influence in the West, but not to the degree they had during the middle ages. In the modern period, the nation-state has been a far more significant factor in shaping human behavior.

Thus there is a reversal of the Hegelian formulation on the relation of ideas and history. For Hegel, the idea was an autonomous teleological concept. The idea has its origins outside the world of human activity. For the poststructuralists, the idea still moves history, but it has its origins in the experiences of the historical beings that possess the capacity to hold ideas.

Therefore, the poststructuralists see our understanding of the world as interpretive. A world in which there are models of knowledge and understanding can only be open to interpretation. There must always be an opening, an alternative explanation, a differing model. The methods of genealogy and deconstruction show the historical and cultural origins of our ideas.

In this sense, poststructuralism may be better at critique than building a positive social and political platform. This criticism is often stated, and has some merit. However, such a positive nihilism, as Foucault puts it, may be the only philosophic space within the materialist understanding of history. Undermining the metaphysical foundations of essentialist ontology, and contextualizing teleological claims to historical inevitability, leaves only the past and present as empirical reference points for analysis. While such a position may be disconcerting, it is the only temporal space in which materialist analysis can be conducted.

This helps explain the significance of *difference* as an ethical posture. Difference is what remains when all the positive statements regarding the subject have been relativized. What is absent is infinite. It opens the possibilities of new ways of conceiving identity and representation in the most general sense.

When it comes to human subjectivity such an approach has a material limit. The empowerment of difference leads to a radical form of individualism. Each must be allowed to explore the conditions of existence and construct their own identities outside of the intrusive essentialism that has become part of institutional existence. Individualism is the default, the condition brought about in the absence of essentialist claims. What is left is the material presence of human beings trying to make sense of their experience.

The critique of essentialist, institutional discourse also creates the basis for a materialist critique of power. This is a form of power that is broader than just forcing compliance with personal or institutional will. This is the power to define the individual which is embedded within all organized social life. This is a form of power which causes individuals to alter their perceptions of self-interest. It is the power that creates common identities and missions that are at the core of social existence. There is always, therefore, some tension between the demands of institutional existence and the ethics of difference.

Nevertheless, the casting of the materiality of power within this framework is a very powerful basis for critique in the contemporary world. It is liberating in a personal as well as a political sense. It erodes the power of the concept of normalcy, allowing people new avenues of personal expression, as well as providing a means by which people and groups can speak back to the institutions of power.

To this point I have focused on areas where poststructuralism has an affinity with the materialist model outlined in chapter 1. However, there are a few areas where there is some contrast, at least in terms of focus. One area in particular stands out. This has to do with the implications of a human-centric view of knowledge. There is little doubt that the poststructuralist view of human knowledge as an exclusively human creation. Following Nietzsche, the claim is that everything we know is from a human point of view.

However, there is an element from both Nietzsche and Darwin regarding significance of this claim for survival that could use greater attention. The natural environment is not a social construction. Our interpretation of it is. Our materiality needs to be seen in the context of the living order of the world more generally. We are not the only species on the planet, and the fate of all species is linked.

The circular nature of textual grafting as a means of legitimizing societal structures and norms diminishes the significance of the natural world and its influences on our material well-being. It is so fixated on the processes of cultural reproduction that the conditions for the material reproduction of our physical presence is less in focus. A pragmatic understanding of this distinction would give poststructuralism and empiricism some common ground.

CONCLUSION

Poststructuralism is a systematic attempt to bring a materialist understanding of consciousness to the continental tradition in philosophy. It is particularly strong in explaining the processes of cultural reproduction, material expression of power, and providing a materialist understanding of the relation of history to individual thought and action. It represents a particular variant of the socio-culture form of materialism.

Poststructuralism also possesses a materialist epistemology. Knowledge is a product of activity that is material both in its premises and in its conclusions. There can be no characterization of transcendent knowledge, no teleological project, no universal construction of the subject that is not reducible to a process of adjusting new experiences within the framework of an existing context. Texts are related to other texts. They are grafts whose legitimacy is related only to their repetition. They are relative to their place and time and, therefore, to the material forces of history out of which they are generated.

These assertions necessitate a broader interpretation of the socio-cultural determinants than those found in the Marxian notion of an institutional superstructure. For the poststructuralists, institutions create their own mechanisms for generating truth claims and are, therefore, not strictly tied to production. The result is an understanding of power that is multi-dimensional in its scope and omnipresent as part of social life. Institutions manifest power as the imposition of identity, the process of circumscribing behavior, norms, and values as part of the process of institutional self-maintenance.

The goal of liberation is not removed from the agenda by the reformulated position. However, resistance to power cannot be legitimated within an ideologically constructed ontology. It is legitimated in epistemological terms. It is the struggle against the imposition of identity. Struggle takes the form of resistance to what deconstruction reveals as arbitrary and contextual. Its method is the creation of counter-discourses within a discursive field made possible by the reconstruction of materialist doctrine.

In the final analysis, the judgment of whether or not poststructuralism qualifies as a materialist doctrine will depend on what one considers the ontological status of *context*. If you cannot directly sense context, can it still constitute a material force in history? It is the position of the poststructuralists that context constitutes the materiality of history in its most general sense, incorporating both the materiality of our bodies and the social constructions that have evolved as part of our history. Context is a material force because it moves history, even if it evades direct sensual contact. We are the products of the complex, interrelated environment, the totality of which escapes definition. Such a context is real, even if its totality is not directly sensed by our sensing apparatus. We see its reality as a force that moves history.

NOTES

1. Plato, "Republic," in *The Collected Dialogues of Plato*, edited by Edith Hamilton and Huntington Cairns (Princeton, NJ: Princeton University Press, 1989) 588.
2. Karl Marx, "The German Ideology," in *The Marx-Engels Reader* (New York: Norton, 1978), 154.
3. Marx, "The German Ideology," 158.
4. Friedrich Engels, "On Morality," in *The Marx-Engels Reader*.
5. Marx, "The German Ideology," 164.

6. See, "Capital" volume 1 in *The Marx-Engels Reader*, 713; and *The Grundrisse*, edited by David McLellan (New York: Harper, 1972), 121.

7. Marx, "Preface," in *A Contribution to the Critique of Political Economy* (New York: International Publishers, 1976).

8. Marx, *The Grundrisse*, 121.

9. Marx, *Capital*, 214.

10. Louis Althusser, "Interview." Quoted in F. Vavarro. *Filosofia y Marxismo: Entrevista a Louis Althusser* (Mexico City: Siglo Veintiuno Editores), 1988.

11. Max Weber, *The Methodology of the Social Sciences* (New York: Free Press, 1949), 103.

12. Jean Baudrillard, "The Mirror of Production," in *Selected Writings* (Palo Alto, CA: Stanford University Press, 1996), 114.

13. Jacques Derrida, *Positions* (Chicago: University of Chicago Press, 1981), 74.

14. Marx, "Manuscripts of 1844," in *The Marx-Engels Reader*, 74-78.

15. Derrida, *Positions*, 63.

16. Louis Althusser and Etienne Balibar, *Reading Capital* (New York: Random House, 1970), 41.

17. Louis Althusser, *On the Reproduction of Capital* (London: Verso, 2014), 77.

18. Althusser, *On the Reproduction of Capital*, 83.

19. Baudrillard, *Selected Writings*, 179.

20. Jean Baudrillard, *Simulations*, (New York: Semiotext, 1983), 87.

21. Jean Baudrillard, *The Vital Illusion* (New York: Columbia University Press, 2000), 21.

22. Baudrillard, *Simulations*, 103.

23. Baudrillard, *Simulations*, 106.

24. Jean Baudrillard, *The Transparency of Evil* (London: Verso, 2000).

25. Baudrillard, *The Vital Illusion*, 21.

26. Baudrillard, *The Impossible Exchange* (New York: Verso, 2001), 5.

27. Friedrich Nietzsche, "On Truth and Lies in a Nonmoral Sense," in *Nietzsche Selections* (New York: Macmillan, 1993), 49.

28. Nietzsche, *The Genealogy of Morals and Ecco Homo* (New York: Vintage, 1989), 26.

29. Nietzsche, *The Will to Power* (New York: Random House, 1967), 14.

30. Gilles Deleuze, *Nietzsche and Philosophy* (New York: Columbia University Press, 1983), 133.

31. Jacques Derrida, *Positions*, 20.

32. Jacques Derrida, *Writing and Difference* (Chicago: University of Chicago Press, 1978), 200-201.

33. Jacques Derrida, *Of Grammatology* (Baltimore: Johns Hopkins University Press, 1976), 6.

34. Derrida, *Positions*, 90.

35. Jacques Derrida, *Dissemination* (Chicago: University of Chicago Press, 1981), 353.

36. Derrida, *Dissemination*, 312.

37. Derrida, *Dissemination*, 355.

38. Derrida, *Dissemination*, 333.

39. Derrida, Dissemination, 300.

40. Derrida. *Positions*, 93.

41. Michel Foucault, *Power/Knowledge* (New York: Pantheon, 1980), 115.

42. Foucault, *Power/Knowledge*, 133.

43. Michel Foucault, "Orders of Discourse," *Social Science Information* 10:2 (1971), 8.

44. Niklas Luhmann, *Social Systems* (Palo Alto: Stanford University Press. 1995).

45. Michel Foucault, "The Subject and Power," in *Beyond Structuralism and Hermeneutics*, edited by Hubert Dreyfus and Paul Rabinow (Chicago: University of Chicago Press, 1983), 212.

46. Michel Foucault, *Language Countermemory and Practice* (Ithaca, NY: Cornell University Press, 1986), 216.

47. Michel Foucault, *The History of Sexuality* (New York: Vintage, 1990).

48. Michel Foucault, *Madness and Civilization* (New York: Vintage, 1965).

49. Foucault, *Power/Knowledge*, 125.
50. Foucault, "On the Genealogy of Ethics," in *Beyond Structuralism and Hermeneutics*, 236.

Conclusion

The World in Human Hands

SUMMARY: MATERIALISM AND METHODS

It is tempting at this point to pronounce the winner in the contest of who is the most materialistic within the continental tradition. I will resist such a temptation. The reason is not that they are all equally materialistic in the approach and understanding, but that they should each be seen as part of an ongoing process of development and adjustment. Each discussion occurs in a different time frame, as part of a different cultural and historical context. For that reason, each of our authors brings something slightly different to the discussion.

Kant is still heavily influenced by the discussion of human nature in which authors seek to define a universal conception of the self that will serve as a foundation for social and political prescriptions. Once the subject has been defined, social and political action is a derivative. Such a characterization must be static, immune from the transformations that take place in the social, natural, or technological environments. Such a method for the construction of the subject cannot be consistent with the dynamic processes that form our understanding of the world.

Yet Kant still brings something important into the discussion. With the idea that the brain processes sensation, Kant has created the space for the mind as the mediator of experience. It is the mind that interprets the world. It does not capture its essence. The mind constructs its picture of reality, an illusion of the real, that allows the human being to function and survive. All in the physical world is known to us only by appearance.

Kant's dualism ultimately creates a problem for its materialist elements. The division of the phenomenal and noumenal does provide Kant the basis for his claims of universal morals and sweeping ethical pronouncements. However, the metaphysics of the noumenal cannot be defended within a materialist world view. Thus, the continental tradition finds itself at a cross-road. One can move in the direction of Hegel and Husserl and try to give foundational substance to the noumenal through metaphysics or one can move in the opposite direction and focus on the material and the transformation of sensations into cognitions as the key to understanding consciousness.

Marx provides the critical first step. By the middle of the nineteenth century evolutionary biology was making its presence felt and the genius of Marx was his ability to comprehend the significance of these ideas for philosophy and social inquiry. If Darwin is correct, everything we know and believe about the world has human origins. The mind creates a cognitive illusion of reality that includes human history, ethics, and human subjectivity, and the prescriptive elements of the social order. These are all fabrications of the mind interacting with the totality of the lived experiences of human beings. There can be no transcendental guidance, not by an omnipotent deity or cosmological idea.

We must look to ourselves and the processes that are part of human existence in order to understand the origin of our interpretations. Marx points to society and culture in a general sense, and to the process of material production more specifically. Human beings must survive in order to make history. The time frame for our social evolution is shorter than that of biological evolution, but it is nonetheless transformative. What is different? In biology the organism is itself transformed as it adjusts to the environment. Social evolution involves human beings transforming the environment to have it meet their needs and desires. Human beings alter the environment in order to enhance their existence. This is carried out by an act of living will, a fusion of cognition about the social and natural world coupled with a determination to exist and thrive.

Marx identifies that nexus and in doing so begins a transformation in the continental tradition. Human beings are motivated by the material necessities of their existence. As a result, they have created ever more efficient forms of productivity, expanded the means of administration and control over ever larger territories of the earth, and created an interpretive understanding of the natural world that has assisted these processes. The system is driven by change. It is historical and dynamic.

But Marx often fails to fully appreciate that in a dynamic system it is impossible to fully articulate the essence of the beings that are influenced by the dynamics of the system. *Essence* is a static concept. For a materialist, there can be no concept of human nature used for normative critique. There can be no teleological conception of history that motivates the process. There can be no single cause of transformation given the vast array of stimuli that enter the domain of human reason. Marx goes beyond the ordinary metaphysics of language in pushing this part of his position.

But despite these problem, Marx has begun something important. He has demonstrated the possibility of conceiving the world as something which is in human hands. Continental philosophy now has a materialist variation.

Max Weber moves further down the road of materialism than is usually recognized. This is the case in two ways. Most common understandings of Weber reflect on his use of empirical data. He engages in studies, gathers statistical data, and brings an empirical edge to the exploration of social matters.

However, there is another materialist side of Weber that comes from his larger methodological framework. Weber stresses the necessity of interpretation. The world is infinitely complex and the only means of grasping it is to try and articulate an understanding that is *causally sufficient* for what the researcher seeks to explain. So in the last chapter of *The Methodology of the Social Sciences* Weber articulates a technique of taking a slice out of reality in order to try and understand the world. Even if this is not identical to the method of Derrida in *Dissemination*, there is something very close to that position in Weber's procedure. The point is that social inquiry is moving in a direction that affords a greater appreciation for the limits of human cognition in a world of infinite stimuli.

What is also striking in Weber's analysis is the means by which social inquiry is validated. In the study of history and culture, knowledge claims must be validated both empirically and empathetically. The experience being described by the investigator must speak to the experience of the listener. This is a central component of Weber's interpretive sociology.

It means that there is always a subjective element in any inquiry into social phenomena. This is not to suggest that there are not facts of history, but that the arrangement of those facts into a causal scheme is an interpretive enterprise. For that reason, there are always potential alternatives interpretations. The world is actually full of competing interpretations. Our cultural struggles over norms and values cannot be separated from these competing narratives. In the final analysis, what we perceive as our ideal and material interest are the material forces of change in the world.

Friedrich Nietzsche also explores the limitations of human cognition. Accepting that we cannot have any transcendental knowledge, Nietzsche sees the world filled with false narratives of human subjectivity and the conditions of human existence. Metaphysics is rejected in favor of a hard, cutting critique of human weakness and limitations. Yet to Nietzsche, the species deludes itself into believing it can commune with the gods and possess their transcendent wisdom.

While human beings build civilization, everything we construct is built on quicksand. Beliefs have no foundation other than repetition. In this sense, there is some similarity to Weber. However, with Nietzsche even the natural sciences represent a reflection of ourselves back to ourselves. Not only are they interpretive in character, but they are human-centric in the most extreme sense. They tell us only what we are capable of understanding. They give us only appearances, never the essential truth that we crave.

So we live our lives according to the illusions of truth that we have constructed for ourselves. There is no escape from this condition. However, there is *Joyful Wisdom* for Nietzsche. It is Nietzsche who wants to dissipate the despair that can infect the culture as a result of a materialist understanding of the world. The loss of foundational truths can leave some adrift, in a condition of anomie and senselessness. Yet despite all the negative elements in Nietzsche's critique of our existence there is one bright ray of hope. Dionysus can set us free. We are free of the camel's burden. We are free to take charge of ourselves in the world.

Much of Nietzsche finds its way into poststructuralism. As Jacques Derrida puts it, Nietzsche is writing in a time before linguistics. It is possible to put Nietzsche's insights into a more contemporary framework and explore the implications of such a position.

To Baudrillard, a world filled with illusion means simulation. We live in a mirage created from the mix of interests, technology, and power. The institutional edifice we have constructed manifests the interests of an elite that seeks to continue the existing structures of power through the maintenance of a narrative that legitimates their domination. The nexus of technological change and the development of the symbolic order reinforce the structure of domination and creates the potential for a dystopian future.

Derrida outlines the means by which the illusions of any era are passed on and transformed. Dissemination is a process of cultural transmission. World views are embedded within language. Language is metaphorical and therefore cannot capture the essence of any object or person. There is only text connecting to other texts back through the span of time.

Derrida's accomplishment is to provide a systematic description of how the process of language and culture regenerate themselves. The legitimacy of those texts comes from their grafting onto existing texts. The illusion takes on the character of the real as the texts are repeated and connected. Thus, what Derrida has explained is a material process among human being by which the symbolic take on the character of the actual through the process of transmission.

For Foucault, this process has serious political implications. The contextual nature of knowledge construction means that our political lives are constructed out of a mixture of institutional power and technological context. Power is everywhere, in all institutional structures. Institutions maintain themselves by generating a self-reinforcing form of knowledge. Institutions do not reflect our essential natures but seek to construct our understanding of subjectivity in a way that legitimates and maintains the existing systems of power and domination.

Foucault also has significant insights regarding the relative and contextual nature of knowledge and the present order of politics. If we live in a historical system that is dynamic, then the relative nature of the present needs to be understood against the material backdrop of history. The modern period and the notion of nation-state sovereignty emerged and reinforced one another. When we step back and look at the present with a materialist understanding of history, we can see both the arbitrary character of present order and the repressive nature of its functions.

MATERIALISM AND NATURE

What Marx understood was the idea that if we begin with the assumption that history means change, and that such changes will affect the thoughts and ideas of beings living within history, then making people conscious of the dynamics of change and its effects on their understanding of the world will liberate them from both the mental chains that confine their thinking and the physical chains that constrain their bodies. Such is the nature of the materialist understanding of the world.

Today we have the linguistic tools to extend the project of human liberation. As Foucault understood, we cannot eliminate power. Society will need to be organized. Collective action will need to be taken. Those that violate the well-being of others will need to be restrained in their actions. However, materialism allows the asking of a different set of questions regarding the nature of social life and the character of human interaction. We no longer need to be constrained by the question, "What is true?" When we accept that we are historical creatures constructing relative and contingent truths we are in a position to ask a different question. We can ask, "How do we choose to live?"

Such a question is possible only within the materialist framework because only materialism put the world squarely in human hands. There is no historical purpose other than that which we assert. There is no method of production or social organization other than that which is constructed by human beings.

Various forms of transcendentalism are seductive. They provide foundational support for a fixed and static understanding of people and life. They often contain pronouncements of agendas and programs that follow from their assumptions. Life has a simplicity about it when directed by stable notions of truth and identity.

However, within a materialist framework, such notions that have appeared throughout history must be abandoned. Not only are their foundational underpinnings epistemologically unsupportable, but they are dangerous in several senses. Much has already been said about the political dangers. A self-referencing system of narratives reflecting the interests of power presents a danger to anyone not living within the dominant structure of subjectivity.

However, there is another danger that emerges from transcendentalism generally. Transcendental claims rely on the division of the human being into mind/matter or soul/body, or some other such claimed bifurcation. The problem is that such a division gives life an illusory character. It reifies a heuristic linguistic metaphor into foundational support for the transcendence of human life, a life which has no direct connection to physical nature.

Such a life is separated from the world. It is independent of the natural conditions of existence and the material necessities that support such an existence. We alter the environment. We change the conditions of life for ourselves and the other species living in the world. We pretend to converse with the gods while we wallow in the cesspool of our own creation. As a species, we will not stop being a threat to ourselves and all the other living species in our world until we extinguish the idea that we are not material beings living in the world

Materialism brings us back into the world. We must engage multiple narratives of life and survival. We need to understand the physicality of existence in order to have a functional understand of our relationship to the world. We must look at the implications of Darwin both for philosophy and life.

My attempt in this work was to show an evolution of thinking about how we understand the world. The continental tradition in philosophy has developed a strongly materialist component. However, this discussion is far from over. The next chapter has yet to be written.

Bibliography

Althusser, Louis and Etienne Balibar. *Reading Capital*. New York: Random House, 1970.
———. "Interview." Quoted in F. Vavarro. *Filosofia y Marxismo: Entrevista a Louis Althusser*. Mexico City: Siglo Veintiuno Editores, 1988.
———. *On the Reproduction of Capitalism*. London: Verso, 2014.
Bacon, Francis. "The Great Instauration." In *English Philosophers from Bacon to Mill*. Ed. by Edwin A. Burtt. New York: Modern Library, 1939.
———. "Novem Organum." In *English Philosophers from Bacon to Mill*. Ed. by Edwin A. Burtt. New York: Modern Library, 1939.
Baudrillard, Jean. *Simulations*. New York: Semiotext, 1983.
———. "The Mirror of Production." In *Jean Baudrillard: Selected Writings*. Palo Alto, CA: Stanford University Press, 1996.
———. "Simulacra and Simulations." In *Jean Baudrillard: Selected Writings*. Palo Alto, CA: Stanford University Press, 1996.
———. *The Transparency of Evil*. London: Verso, 1999.
———. *The Vital Illusion*. New York: Columbia University Press, 2000.
———. *The Impossible Exchange*. New York: Verso, 2001.
Braidotti, Rosi. "The Politics of Life Itself and New Ways of Dying." In *New Materialisms*. Ed. by Diana Coole and Samantha Frost. Durham, NC: Duke University Press, 2010.
Cheah, Pheng, "Non-Dialectical Materialism." In *New Materialisms*. Ed. by Diana Coole and Samantha Frost. Durham, NC: Duke University Press, 2010.
Darwin, Charles. *On the Origin of Species*. Philadelphia: University of Pennsylvania Press, 1959.
Deleuze, Gilles. *Nietzsche and Philosophy*. New York: Columbia University Press, 1983.
Derrida, Jacques. *Of Grammatology*. Baltimore: Johns Hopkins University Press, 1976.
———. *Writing and Difference*. Chicago: University of Chicago Press, 1978.
———. *Positions*. Chicago: University of Chicago Press, 1981.
———. *Dissemination*. Chicago: University of Chicago Press, 1981.
———. Specters of Marx. New York: Routledge, 1994.
Descartes, Rene. *A Discourse on Method*. London: J. M. Dent and Sons, 1941.
Dewey, John, *The Influence of Darwin on Philosophy*. New York: Henry Holt and Company, 1910.
Engels, Friedrich. "Speech at the Graveside of Karl Marx." *In The Marx-Engels Reader*. Ed. by Robert Tucker. New York: Norton, 1978.
———. "On Morality" *In The Marx-Engels Reader*. Ed. by Robert Tucker. New York: Norton, 1978.

Feuerbach, Ludwig, "Principles of the Philosophy of the Future." In *The Fiery Brook: Selected Writings of Ludwig Feuerbach*. Garden City, NY: Doubleday and Company, 1978.

Foucault, Michel. *Madness and Civilization*. New York: Vintage, 1965.

———. "Orders of Discourse," In *Social Science Information* 10:2, 1971.

———. *Power/Knowledge*. New York: Pantheon, 1980.

———. "The Subject and Power." In *Beyond Structuralism and Hermeneutics*, by Hubert Dreyfus and Paul Rabinow. Chicago: University of Chicago Press, 1983.

———. "On the Genealogy of Ethics." In *Beyond Structuralism and Hermeneutics*, by Hubert Dreyfus and Paul Rabinow. Chicago: University of Chicago Press, 1983.

———. *Language Countermemory and Practice*. Ithaca, NY: Cornell University Press, 1986.

———. *The History of Sexuality*. New York: Vintage, 1990.

Hall, John. "Max Weber's Methodological Strategy and Comparative Lifeworld Phenomenology." *Human Studies* 4:2 1981.

Hegel, Georg, W. F. *The Philosophy of History*. New York: Dover, 1956.

———. *Phenomenology of the Mind*. New York: Harper and Row, 1967.

Henry, Michel. *Material Phenomenology*. New York: Fordham University Press, 2008.

Hume, David. "An Abstract of a Treatise of Human Nature." In *On Human Nature and the Understanding*. Ed. by Antony Flew. New York: Collier-Macmillan, 1971.

———. "An Inquiry Concerning Human Understanding." In *On Human Nature and the Understanding*. Ed. by Antony Flew. New York: Collier-Macmillan, 1971.

———. "A Treatise of Human Nature." In *On Human Nature and the Understanding*. Ed. by Antony Flew. New York: Collier-Macmillan, 1971.

Husserl, Edmund. *Phenomenology and the Crisis in Philosophy*. New York: Harper, 1965.

Kant, Immanuel. *The Critique of Pure Reason*. New York: Random House, 1958.

———. *The Metaphysical Elements of Justice*. Indianapolis: Bobbs-Merrill, 1965.

———. "Intoduction to *The Critique of Pure Reason*." In *The Philosophy of Kant*. Ed. by Carl J. Friedrich. New York: Modern Library, 1977.

———. "The Metaphysical Foundation of Morals." In *The Philosophy of Kant*. Ed. by Carl J. Friedrich. New York: Modern Library, 1977.

———. "The Critique of Judgment." In *The Philosophy of Kant*. Ed. by Carl J. Friedrich. New York: Modern Library, 1977.

Koch, Andrew M. *Romance and Reason: Ontological and Social Sources of Alienation in the Writings of Max Weber*. Lanham: Roman and Littlefield (Lexington), 2006.

Koch, Andrew M., and Zeddy, Amanda. *Democracy and Domination: Technologies of Integration and the Rise of Collective Power*. Lanham, MD: Lexington Books, 2009.

Lange, F. A. *The History of Materialism*. New York: Harcourt Brace and Company, 1925.

Luhmann, Niklas. *Social Systems*. Palo Alto, CA: Stanford University Press. 1995.

Lukes, Steven. *Marxism and Morality*. Oxford, UK: Oxford University Press, 1987.

Marx, Karl. *A Contribution to the Critique of Political Economy*. Edited by Maurice Dobb. New York: International Publishers, 1970.

———. *The Grundrisse*, edited by David McLellan. New York: Harper, 1972.

———. *Capital*. New York: Dutton Publishing, 1974.

———. "Thesis on Feuerbach." In *The Marx-Engels Reader*. Ed. by Robert Tucker. New York: Norton, 1978.

———. "Economic and Philosophic Manuscripts of 1844." In *The Marx-Engels Reader*. Ed. by Robert Tucker. New York: Norton, 1978.

———. "Contribution to the Critique of Hegel's Philosophy of Right." In *The Marx-Engels Reader*. Ed. by Robert Tucker. New York: Norton, 1978.

———. "The German Ideology." In *The Marx-Engels Reader*. Ed. by Robert Tucker. New York: Norton, 1978.

———. "The Holy Family." In *Karl Marx: Selected Writings*. Ed. by David McLellan. Oxford, UK: Oxford University Press, 1985.

———. "Capital." In *The Marx-Engels Reader*. Ed. by Robert Tucker. New York: Norton, 1978.

———. "Wage Labor and Capital." In *The Marx-Engels Reader*. Ed. by Robert Tucker. New York: Norton, 1978.

————. "The Communist Manifesto." In *The Marx-Engels Reader*. Ed. by Robert Tucker. New York: Norton, 1978.

Nietzsche, Friedrich. "The Anti-Christ." In *The Portable Nietzsche*. New York: Viking Press, 1954.

————. "The Birth of Tragedy." In *The Birth of Tragedy and The Genealogy of Morals*, edited by Francis Golffing. Garden City, NJ: Doubleday Anchor, 1956.

————. *Beyond Good and Evil*. New York: Vintage, 1966.

————. *The Will to Power*. New York: Random House, 1967.

————. *Thus Spoke Zarathustra*. Middlesex, England: Penguin Books, 1971.

————. *The Gay Science*. New York: Vintage, 1974.

————. *On the Genealogy of Morals and Ecce Homo*. New York: Vintage, 1989.

————. "Joyful Wisdom." In *Nietzsche Selections*, Ed. by Richard Schacht. New York: Scribner/Macmillan, 1993.

————. "On Truth and Lies in a Nonmoral Sense." In *Nietzsche Selections*, Ed. by Richard Schacht. New York: Scribner/Macmillan, 1993.

————. "Twilight of the Idols." In *Nietzsche Selections*, Ed. by Richard Schacht. New York: Scribner/Macmillan, 1993.

Plato. "Republic," In *The Collected Dialogues of Plato*, Ed. by Edith Hamilton and Huntington Cairns. Princeton, NJ: Princeton University Press, 1989

Weber, Max. "Science as a Vocation." In *From Max Weber*. Ed. by Hans H. Gerth and C. Wright Mills. Oxford, UK: Oxford University Press, 1946.

————. "The Social Psychology of the World Religions" In *From Max Weber*. Ed. by Hans H. Gerth and C. Wright Mills. Oxford, UK: Oxford University Press, 1946.

————. "Politics as a Vocation." In *From Max Weber*. Ed. by Hans H. Gerth and C. Wright Mills. Oxford: Oxford University Press, 1946.

————. "Religious Rejections of the World and Their Directions." In *From Max Weber*. Ed. by Hans H. Gerth and C. Wright Mills. Oxford: Oxford University Press, 1946.

————. *The Methodology of the Social Sciences*. Ed. by Edward A. Shils and Henry A. Finch. New York: Free Press, 1949.

————. *Roscher and Knies: The Logical Problems of Historical Economics*. New York: Free Press, 1975.

————. *Economy and Society*. Berkeley: University of California Press, 1978.

————. "The Nation State and Economic Policy." In *Weber: Political Writings*. Ed by Peter Lassman and Ronald Speirs. Cambridge, UK: Cambridge University Press, 1994.

Index

absolute spirit. *See* God
action/activity, x, 11–12, 41, 71, 72, 74, 76,
    79, 92, 100, 117, 120, 127; collective,
    5, 16, 58, 71, 74, 76, 77, 78, 131;
    human, x, 1, 12, 45, 51, 70, 73, 91, 94,
    102, 106, 107, 117, 121, 122;
    individual, 49, 72, 76, 123; life as, xi,
    45, 46, 49, 50, 59, 93; Marx, on, 44, 49,
    50, 67; morality, 32, 34, 35, 93;
    productive, 57, 108, 123; sensual, 44,
    49, 51, 53, 59; social, 5, 14, 70, 71, 74,
    77, 78, 110. *See also* Aquinas, Saint
    Thomas; history; human; morality
Althusser, Louis, 3, 9, 15, 97, 110–111;
    ideological state apparatus, 111; on
    Marx, 17, 64, 105, 108–109, 110, 111,
    121; *Structural Marxism*, 5. *See also*
    subjectivity
animals, 92, 99, 100, 101
anthropomorphism, 97, 98, 102, 106, 114
The Archeology of Knowledge. *See*
    Foucault
Aristotle, 1, 13, 29
Augustine, Saint, 1
Aquinas, Saint Thomas, 1

Bacon, Sir Francis, vii, 2, 22, 23, 23–25,
    52; "Great Instauration", 23; on
    inductive logic, 10, 52; "Novum
    Organum", 23

Baudrillard, Jean, xii, 64, 105, 109, 130;
    "The Orders of Simulacra", 112. *See
    also* the code; "the real"; relativism
becoming, 99, 99–100, 100
being. *See* essence
belief, 5, 89
Bentham, Jeremy, 54
biology. *See* natural science
bourgeoisie, 54–55, 55, 56, 57, 58, 60, 96,
    97, 98, 113, 130
Braidotti, Rosi, 9. *See also* vitalism
bureaucracy. *See* institutionalism

capitalism, 45, 46, 47, 52–53, 54, 57, 60,
    66, 78, 80, 108, 110; exchange-value,
    54; and history, 55, 57, 108; laws of,
    54, 57. *See also* law; and materialism,
    55; supply and demand, 46, 54; surplus
    value, 46, 54, 55–56, 108; use-value,
    54; production; labor
Capital. *See* Marx
categorical imperative, 32, 33, 36, 42, 96
causality, 4, 27, 30, 31, 32, 47, 63, 65, 69,
    79, 129; Marx on, 51, 53, 54; and
    materialism, 10, 37, 61, 71; Weber on,
    64, 67, 68, 69, 70, 72, 82
change, 16, 51, 71, 76, 97, 110, 114, 121,
    128; revolutionary, 57, 60, 77, 108; and
    society, 15, 76, 98. *See also*
    evolutionary biology; force: material;
    history

About the Author

Andrew M. Koch is a professor of political philosophy in the Department of Government and Justice Studies at Appalachian State University. He received his PhD from the University of California at Santa Barbara and is a former Fulbright Scholar and Friedrich Ebert Foundation Fellow. His main area of research is continental epistemology and philosophy. Among his published works are *Medieval America*; *Democracy and Domination*; *Poststructuralism and the Politics of Method*; *Romance and Reason: Ontological and Social Sources of Alienation in the Writings of Max Weber*; *Knowledge and Social Construction*; *Poststructuralism and the Epistemological Basis of Anarchism*; and *Cyber Citizen or Cyborg Citizen: The Problem of Political Agency in Virtual Politics*.

www.ingramcontent.com/pod-product-compliance
Lightning Source LLC
Chambersburg PA
CBHW021820270326
41932CB00007B/267